To

Nancy Pritchard,

With best wishes,

Frederick J. Luhmann

CALL
and
RESPONSE

ORDAINING
MARRIED
MEN AS
CATHOLIC
PRIESTS

Frederick J. Luhmann

Call and Response

ORDAINING
MARRIED
MEN AS
CATHOLIC PRIESTS

Library of Congress Cataloging-in Publication Data
Luhmann, Frederick J.
Call and Response: Ordaining Married Men as
Catholic Priests p. cm.
1. Scripture, 2. Canons of Church Councils, 3. Pastoral
Provisions: United States, Canada, England and Wales,
4. Eastern Churches, 5. Canon Law West and East,
6. Case Examples, 7. Data, 8. Future Options
Includes Major Documents: Text and List.

ISBN: 0-9718217-0-4
Library of Congress Control Number: 2002090560

Published by: Dialogue Press
              303 Ashby Court
              Berryville, VA 22611-1406
              (540) 955-9109
              email: Dialogue Press@aol.com

Printed in the United States by:
Morris Publishing
3212 East Highway 30 * Kearney NE 68847
1-800-650-7888

Peter

*Fisherman, Spouse, Parent,
Apostle, Priest, Pope, Martyr,
and Model
for
All Who Hear
the Call and Respond*

When they had finished breakfast, Jesus said to Simon Peter, "Simon, son of John, do you love me more than these?" He said to him, "Yes, Lord, you know that I love you." He said to him, "Feed my lambs." He then said to him a second time, "Simon, son of John, do you love me?" He said to him, "Yes, Lord, you know that I love you." He said to him, "Tend my sheep." He said to him a third time, "Simon, son of John, do you love me?" Peter was distressed that he had said to him a third time, "Do you love me?" and he said to him, "Lord, you know everything; you know that I love you." [Jesus] said to him, "Feed my sheep." (Jn 21:15-17)

In Memory

**Most Reverend Raymond A. Lucker, D.D.
February 24, 1927 - September 19, 2001**

Ordination of Married Men

I believe that we ought to change the law and have the option of married clergy.

I think we need to pray over the issue, discuss it, and see if there wouldn't be some way to begin to have the ordination of married men.

I bring up this issue because of my concern for the church, because of my love for the church, and because I believe the Eucharist and the celebration of the sacraments is at the very heart of what we are as a church. We need ordained clergy for that. But there is a church law in the way of fulfilling the law of God.

I believe so much in the centrality of the Eucharist, and in light of this we need to consider the issue of obligatory celibacy of the clergy.

Pastoral Letter, October 1998

TABLE OF CONTENTS

YESTERDAY

TODAY

TOMORROW

EPILOGUE

YESTERDAY

Chapter 1

THE CALL OF THE FIRST DISCIPLES

The young man drew no attention as he walked along in the early blush of morning. At his feet water rolled gently to the shore in a rhythm of sun-speckled ripples, paused for a moment and receded in thin beards of white foam. In the distance two boats punctuated the line of sand and water.

He strolled toward the first boat which rode the undulating swell of water a stone's throw from shore. Aboard, two men stripped to their waists busily hoisted a heavy fish net, cast it in a wide arch and watched it settle into the sea.

As the fishermen rested against the mast, the young man called out from the shore, "Come after me, and I will make you fishers of men."

The two startled men — brothers, Simon (later called Peter) and Andrew — looked to one another, nodded slightly, and put their backs into retrieving the net. Once ashore, they left the boat beached on the sand and fell silently in step with the young man whose call resonated in their hearts in a way too deep to express in words.

Farther along, the young man stopped at the second boat. Simon and Andrew knew the owner, Zebedee, and his two sons, James and John. The three men raised their eyes briefly from the task of mending their nets to greet their fellow fishermen and the young stranger with them.

The unknown man drew close to the boat, looked into the eyes of the two sons and spoke warmly, "Come follow me."

The brothers at once leapt the short distance to the sand, waved to their father and joined the small band as the young man led the way to his place of residence.

Throughout the night the four recruits listened with respect and awe to the words of the young man who identified himself as Jesus of Nazareth. Each listener felt that in responding to the invitation of this teacher who taught as no man ever had before that his life had changed forever. (Mt 4:18-22, Mk 1:16-20, Lk 5:1-11, Lk 5:27-29, Jn 1:35-42).

The next day on the way to Galilee Jesus continued the education of his new disciples as they passed through the dusty villages along the road. In Galilee, Jesus approached a man named Philip who was from Bethsaida, the hometown of Peter and Andrew. Again, Jesus extended his simple invitation: "Follow me." (Jn 1:43-51)

2

Philip not only accepted the invitation, in his enthusiasm he hastened off to tell his friend Nathanael. "We have found the one about whom Moses wrote in the law, and also the prophets, Jesus son of Joseph, from Nazareth."

Skeptical by nature, Nathanael asked with a note of sarcasm, "Can anything good come from Nazareth?"

Undeterred, Philip said to him, "Come and see."

As a favor to his friend, Nathanael followed Philip to Jesus. When Nathanael approached, Jesus said to those about him, "Here is a true Israelite. There is no duplicity in him."

Nathanael, doubtful, asked, "How do you know me?"

Jesus answered, "Before Philip called you, I saw you under the fig tree."

That was enough for Nathanael. He was convinced that this was no ordinary man. "Rabbi," he said, "you are the Son of God; you are the King of Israel."

After that, some time passed before another unlikely candidate was added to the close-knit band of followers. In one of the towns through which Jesus passed he came upon a man sitting at the customs post, a euphemistic manner of describing one who served as a tax collector for the hated Roman oppressors.

Unbound by social mores, once again, Jesus extended his simple, yet compelling, invitation "Follow me." As did the others, the man named Matthew rose at once and followed Jesus. (Mt 9:9)

To this point, among the first seven followers of Jesus we find four fishermen, a tax collector, an enthusiastic fellow of undetermined background, and a dreamer given to sitting under fig trees. What did they share in common? Why does history record these men among all others as the first followers of Jesus? Each shared common gender and ethnic identity as Jewish males. However, those characteristics hardly explain their instant and total readiness to follow Jesus. How do we understand the phenomenon of grown men abruptly leaving all to follow an itinerant teacher about whom they knew nothing? What was the nature of the spiritual experience they underwent? They each had been singled out and called personally by Jesus. Each had responded immediately and wholeheartedly to that call.

Therein lay the mystery, then and now, of a vocation: The call of Jesus to an individual to follow him without reservation and the accepting response in faith by the individual.

At some point Jesus assembled a core group of followers to whom he gave the name of "apostles." Scripture recounts that after a night of prayer on the mountain Jesus called all of his disciples to him. From among them he chose the twelve apostles: Simon, whom he named Peter, and his brother Andrew, James, John, Philip, Bartholomew, Matthew, Thomas, James the son of Alpheus, Simon, who was called a Zealot, and Judas the son of James, and Judas Iscariot, who became a traitor. (Lk 6:12-16)

On an unnamed hillside the apostles entered into a new plane of relationship with Jesus. They were called to an intimacy which at the time they did not understand or appreciate. Where Jesus went, they went; where he slept, they slept; what he ate, they ate. Each day they absorbed his teachings to doctors of the law in synagogues, to clusters of

4

eager listeners in towns, and to throngs of people pressing upon one another in open fields to hear his words. They looked on as he embraced the poor, cured the sick, comforted the sorrowful, and often drew apart to pray through the night.

When Jesus chose the apostles, he enrolled them as students in the first peripatetic seminary of the new dispensation, a seminary where he was the sole master teacher. Throughout his public ministry he taught and formed them in anticipation of the time when he would send them as his witnesses in Jerusalem, throughout Judea and Samaria, and to the ends of the earth. (Acts 1:8)

On the night before his death, Jesus completed the process which he had begun years earlier with the first call to Andrew and Peter. At the Last Supper he instituted the Eucharist and appointed the apostles to the ministerial priesthood.

> When the hour came, he took his place at the table with the apostles. He said to them, "I have eagerly desired to eat this Passover with you before I suffer, for I tell you, I shall not eat it [again] until there is fulfillment in the kingdom of God." Then he took a cup, gave thanks, and said, "Take this and share it among yourselves; for I tell you [that] from this time on I shall not drink of the fruit of the vine until the kingdom of God comes." Then he took the bread, said the blessing, broke it, and gave it to them, saying, "This is my body, which will be given for you; **do this in memory of me.**" And likewise the cup after they had eaten, saying, "This cup is the new covenant in my blood, which will be shed for you." (Lk 22:14-20)

PRIESTHOOD, CELIBACY, MARRIAGE

Each Christian by virtue of baptism shares in the priesthood of Jesus. However, among all the priestly people of God some are called to a particular vocation of ministerial priesthood. It is to these Christians, singled out by the sacrament of ordination, that by custom the title of "priest" is reserved. Following in direct succession to the apostles, priests reenact among us the Eucharistic sacrifice willed by Christ to be shared by his disciples for all time.

THE TEACHING OF JESUS

The teaching of Jesus on the subject of priesthood and marital status is quite clear. Jesus did not consider either marriage or celibacy in selecting each of the apostles, those whom he would appoint as the first priests of the new dispensation.

Evidence of Peter's married status is provided in Mt 8:14-15.

> Jesus entered the house of Peter, and saw his mother-in-law lying in bed with a fever. He touched her hand, the fever left her, and she rose and waited on him.

A second verification of the fact that Peter was married is found in 1 Cor 9:5 which is discussed in the next section. The scriptural witness of Peter's marriage provides evidence that there is neither a dogmatic nor a disciplinary foundation attributable to Jesus which prohibits the concurrent exercise of the sacramental vocations of marriage and priesthood.

6

The gospels do not provide equivalent clarity of marital status for the other apostles.

In the case of one other apostle there is a gospel record which may be useful for the present discussion. Lk 5:27-29 describes the call of Levi (Matthew) as follows:

> After this he went out and saw a tax collector named Levi sitting at the customs post. He said to him, "Follow me." And leaving everything behind, he got up and followed him. Then Levi gave a great banquet for him in his house, and a large crowd of tax collectors and others were at table with them.

Levi provided not just a simple meal, but a great banquet. Obviously, he was a man of means and mature age, someone of status in the community who had many friends and a house large enough to accommodate a great banquet. Since the average marriage age for males at the time was between 22 and 24 years old,[1] and since Jewish society placed a high regard upon marriage and family life, it is not rash to suggest the likelihood that Levi was married.

In the introduction to this section the statement is made that Jesus considered neither marriage nor celibacy as a criterion in the choice of his apostles. Could one offer another possibility, namely, that Jesus did not know the marital status of the apostles at the time that he called each to follow him?

Quite simply, No! Such an assumption is inconceivable. Indeed, the gospel accounts may seem to present the initial encounters of Jesus with Andrew, Simon, James, John, Philip and Matthew as casual, almost accidental. One might imagine that if Jesus had walked along the shore at a different location or time of day some other fishermen might just as easily have received the invitation "Come, follow me." That is not the case as is immediately clear from the encounter between Jesus and Nathanael.

Before Nathanael, the skeptic, ever came with Philip, Jesus had seen him sitting under the fig tree. More than that, as Nathanael approaches, Jesus informs the surrounding crowd that he is a true Israelite, a man without duplicity. Jesus surely would have known with equal insight the character of each man he chose to be an apostle and he would have been fully aware that Peter, and perhaps Matthew and others of the future apostles, were married family men. While possessing such knowledge, Jesus never gave an indication that marital status was an impediment to apostleship or priestly ministry.

Any discussion of the marital status of the apostles, of course, must be understood in the context of the teachings of Jesus on marriage and virginity found in the gospel of Matthew.

In reply to some Pharisees who tested him by asking whether it was lawful for a man to divorce his wife for any cause whatever, Jesus replied:

> "Have you not read that from the beginning the Creator 'made them male and female' and said, 'For this reason a man shall leave his father and mother and be joined to his wife, and the two shall become one flesh'? So they are no longer two, but one flesh. Therefore, what God has joined together, no human being must separate." (Mt 19:4-6)

His still apprentice disciples found this teaching of Jesus so hard that they said to him:

> "If that is the case of a man with his wife, it is better not to marry." He answered, "Not all can accept [this] word, but only those to whom it is granted. Some are incapable of marriage because they were born so; some, because they were made so by others; some, because they have renounced marriage for the sake of the kingdom of heaven. Whoever can accept this ought to." (Mt 19:10-12)

Some would find in this passage justification to suggest that the "celibacy" of those who have rejected marriage "for the sake of the kingdom" is in itself a higher spiritual state than is the state of "marriage." Is not the more important condition the motive for the choice, rather than the choice itself? If *celibacy* is chosen for the sake of the kingdom as a state of life, whether as a lay person, religious, or priest, it most certainly witnesses to an openness to grace and constitutes a public sign of commitment to discipleship.

Might it not be said, as well, without violence to the words of Jesus that *marriage* chosen for the sake of the kingdom as a state of life constitutes no less a witness to an openness to grace and constitutes no less a public sign of commitment to discipleship?

In a choice of celibacy or marriage, motive is all important.

Jesus in this passage invites those who can do so to accept the call to a celibate life. His invitation, however, in no way negates the sanctifying nature of a married life, nor does it create a type of spiritual class system with celibacy as a state of life higher than marriage. Indeed, he instituted marriage, not celibacy, as a sacrament.

ACTS AND EPISTLES

In the days and weeks that followed the crucifixion, the apostles experienced emotional waves of grief and despair at the death of Jesus, initial doubt followed by boundless joy and awe at his resurrection, and a shadow of uncertainty for the future as they watched him ascend to the heavens. As yet they could not fully understand the import of all that so recently had taken place. Their number reduced to eleven with the defection of Judas, they retreated to the security of the upper room where together with some women, Mary the mother of Jesus and his brothers they devoted themselves to prayer as they awaited the Spirit whom Jesus had promised would come and bestow power upon them.

Never one to remain inactive too long, after a few days Peter felt the need to demonstrate the leadership which Jesus had entrusted to him. He stood up in the midst of the group of about one hundred and twenty persons and announced that it was time to select a successor to Judas.

> "Therefore, it is necessary that one of the men who accompanied us the whole time the Lord Jesus came and went among us, beginning from the baptism of John until the day on which he was taken up from us, become with us a witness of his resurrection." (Acts 1:21-22)

Two candidates were put forward, Joseph called Barsabbas, who was also known as Justus, and Matthias. After praying, they gave lots to them, and the lot fell upon Matthias, who from that moment forward was counted as one of the apostles.

Two thoughts come to mind in reading this account of the selection of Matthias. Until this moment there has been no mention of him as a follower of Jesus from the beginning. How many others among the one hundred and twenty people in the upper room qualified as candidates under that criterion?

What we know is that in the upper room two candidates "were put forward," the assembled group prayed, the candidates were given lots, and Matthias was chosen. At first the whole affair appears far removed from the process by which Jesus called Andrew, Peter and the others, and then personally chose them as apostles. But is it really so different?

Matthias and Justus satisfied the prerequisite which Peter announced. Each had been a disciple of Jesus from the beginning until his ascension. Each had experienced a "call" to follow Jesus. Whether the call was audible or an interior stirring of the heart did not matter. Each had a choice whether or not to commit his life to Jesus in the intimate relationship of a disciple. The call respected each man's freedom. Each had to choose: to accept the call, as did Andrew, Peter and the other disciples; or to decline and walk away, as did the rich young man who was unable to free himself from the bonds of his possessions in order to follow Jesus. (Mt 19:21-22) Matthias and Justus each gave an affirmative "response" to the call to discipleship, and, in the case of Matthias, subsequently to the status of apostle.

For all Christians through the ages who have been called to the vocations of marriage, lay celibacy, religious life, or sacramental priesthood, Matthias stands as an understandable and encouraging model of one who receives a call to follow Jesus in the secret recesses of the heart and who responds by an interior and unheralded assent.

11

For his own purposes Jesus at any time may reveal himself in an extraordinary manner and/or personally deliver his call vocally to an individual, but most Christians do not receive their vocations as did Saul of Tarsus.

> On his journey, as he was nearing Damascus, a light from the sky suddenly flashed around him. He fell to the ground and heard a voice saying to him, "Saul, Saul, why are you persecuting me?" He said, "Who are you, sir?" The reply came, "I am Jesus, whom you are persecuting. Now get up and go into the city and you will be told what you must do." (Acts 9:3-6)

Obediently, Saul, who was blinded by the light, got up and was led into Damascus. In the city, a disciple named Ananias had a vision in which the Lord told him to go and restore Saul's sight. As soon as Ananias laid his hands on Saul, scales fell from Saul's eyes, and he got up and was baptized.

As the most eloquent and widely traveled of the earliest witnesses of the gospel, Paul's teaching has assumed a unique place in the history of Christian theology. Therefore, it is important to consider Paul's teachings about marriage and celibacy and to reflect on their relationship to priesthood.

The following texts from Paul provide a basis for consideration.

> 1. Now in regard to the matters about which we wrote: "It is a good thing for man not to touch a woman," but because of cases of immorality every man should have his own wife, and every woman her own husband . . .

Do not deprive each other, except perhaps by mutual consent for a time, to be free for prayer, but then return to one another, so that Satan may not tempt you through your lack of self-control. This I say by way of concession, however, not as a command. Indeed, I wish everyone to be as I am, but each has a particular gift from God, one of one kind and one of another.

Now to the unmarried and to widows I say: it is a good thing for them to remain as they are, as I do, but if they cannot exercise self-control they should marry, for it is better to marry than to be on fire. (1Cor 7:1-9)

If one were to find the parchment of this text in a bottle washed up on the seashore, there would be little doubt about Paul's thoughts on marriage and celibacy. Marriage is a necessity because of our lustful nature. Paul concedes this fact with some reluctance. He sets his own celibacy as the ideal while recognizing that each of us has a particular gift from God and that for some marriage is better than "to be on fire." Paul's distorted view of marriage does not reflect the nature of the sanctifying vocation of marriage blessed as a sacrament by Jesus.

2. I should like you to be free of anxieties. An unmarried man is anxious about the things of the Lord, how he may please the Lord. But a married man is anxious about the things of the world, how he may please his wife, and he is divided . . . I am telling you this for your own benefit, not to impose a restraint upon you, but for the sake of propriety and adherence to the Lord without distraction. (1 Cor 7:32-35)

Unfortunately, once again in this text Paul communicates his disdain for marriage. Marriage is a source of anxiety and distraction, while the heart of the unmarried man has but one anxiety — how to serve the Lord. A married man focuses entirely — so it seems — upon the things of the world and on pleasing his wife, things about which an unmarried man has no concern. Perhaps so, if one believes that unmarried men do not have personal goals in life, do not have to earn a living, are not engaged in politics, never allow themselves any personal interests, or pleasures.

It appears that, in his concern to stress the higher calling of celibacy, Paul allows himself to misrepresent the reality of the world in which we live. Unfortunately, his words taken out of context may easily be used to imply that celibacy is the preferred, or even the only, state of life for a person who wishes to adhere to and to serve the Lord without distraction.

> 3. Do we not have a right to take along a Christian wife, as do the rest of the apostles, and the brothers of the Lord and Kephas?
> (1 Cor 9:5)

In this text Paul asserts his equality to Kephas (Peter) and the other apostles. In so doing, however, he provides confirmation not only that Peter was married, but that the other apostles also were married, and, importantly, that Peter and the others were accompanied on their journeys by their wives. Leaving aside the question of whether Paul meant that all, or only some, of the other apostles were married, his testimony confirms that no contradiction exists between the dual sacred vocations of priesthood and marriage.

4. This saying is trustworthy: whoever aspires to the office of bishop desires a noble task. Therefore, a bishop must be irreproachable, married only once, temperate, self-controlled, decent, hospitable, able to teach, not a drunkard, not aggressive, but gentle, not contentious, not a lover of money. He must manage his own household well, keeping his children under control with perfect dignity; for if a man does not know how to manage his own household, how can he take care of the church of God? *(1Tim 3:1-5)*

This text is of particular interest because it clearly confirms that marriage not only is permissible for bishops but, at the very least, might be very desirable: ". . . for if a man does not know how to manage his own household, how can he take care of the church of God?"

CALL AND RESPONSE

Chapter 2

THE CHURCH COUNCILS

Knowledge of the first centuries of Christianity consists largely of shards of information collected from the gospels, acts of the apostles, epistles, secular records, patristic writings, tradition and legend. The resulting historical puzzle includes jagged bits and pieces of fact and fiction bordering vacant blocks of total ignorance. From these limited sources historians diligently seek to construct a composite picture of the early years of the Christian Era. However, our present purpose is more limited, to trace only one subject using information from already well-researched sources.

Chapter 1 confirms that Christ personally established a priesthood which was based upon criteria other than marital status. Additionally, Paul's words about bishops and marriage found in 1 Timothy 3 provide unequivocal testimony that priestly ministry and marriage are compatible.

Other than the scriptural references which have been cited, no other first-century information exists to shed light on the permissibility or prohibition of marriage for bishops and priests. Understandably, the young church had on its mind more pressing matters to consider, including carrying out the last command of Christ:

"Go, therefore, and make disciples of all
nations, baptizing them in the name of the
Father, and of the Son, and of the holy Spirit,
teaching them to observe all that I have
commanded you." (Mt 28:19-20)

On the immediate level, the apostles had to contend
with other concerns, such as the persecution begun by Herod
Aprippa I which resulted in the martyrdom of James the
Greater, and the basic theological issue which Paul brought
before the Council of Apostles regarding the obligation of
pagan converts to observe the requirements of the Old Law.
The marriage or celibacy of clerics was not an agenda item in
the first century, or for some time thereafter.

The second and third centuries passed, as did the first,
with no apparent need to reconsider the generally accepted
permissibility of marriage for bishops and priests. However,
two significant observations concerning Peter deserve
mention. Clement of Alexandria notes that Peter not only
was married but had children. He also passes on the tradition
that Peter's wife suffered martyrdom.[2] Eusebius accepts and
incorporates these facts in his history of the church.[3]

Clement gives further testimony of a more general
nature. After offering commentary on St. Paul's praise of the
life of celibacy, Clement writes as follows:

"All the same, the Church fully receives the
husband of one wife whether he be priest or
deacon or layman, supposing always that he
uses his marriage blamelessly, and such a one
shall be saved in the begetting of children."[4]

An insight into the marital status of another apostle is
given by bishop Polycrates of Ephesus in a letter which he

wrote to St. Victor about 189-190. Polycrates writes that on the last day the Lord will seek "Philip, one of the Twelve Apostles, who is buried in Hieropolis with his two daughters, who grew old as virgins," and a third daughter, who "led a life in the Holy Ghost and rests in Ephasus."[5]

Further examples seem unnecessary in light of the acknowledgments offered by the Second Vatican Council and Pope Paul VI in recent years.

In *Sacerdotalis caelibatus* (June 24, 1967)[6] Paul VI writes:

5. . . . Jesus Himself did not make it [celibacy] a prerequisite in His choice of the Twelve, nor did the Apostles for those who presided over the first Christian communities.

17. Virginity undoubtedly, as the Second Vatican Council declared, "is not, of course, required by the nature of the priesthood itself. This is clear from the practice of the early Church and the tradition of the Eastern Churches."

Given the consensus that there is nothing in the scriptures which requires priestly celibacy and the undisputed history through the third century of a free choice in the matter of marriage, one is inclined to ask:

When and why did the present strict rule of celibacy come into existence?

In order to seek an answer to this question which has great significance, it is necessary to begin with the obvious, namely, that the church of the early centuries, just as the church of today, existed within and was greatly influenced by the socio-political environment within which it found itself.

Since the time of the apostles, the church had spread in all directions to regions far removed from Jerusalem and had embraced large numbers of converts from widely diverse cultures and societies. At times the church experienced shorter or longer periods of peace and prosperity only to be followed by a series of more or less harsh persecutions. The last, and most terrible of all the persecutions, took place in 303 under Diocletian who reigned from 284 to 305.

COUNCIL OF ELVIRA (C. 305)

At about the time of the last persecution a regional council took place in Elvira, a Spanish region near the present-day city of Granada. It is not known when or by whom Christianity was introduced into Spain. Paul had expressed an intent to visit Spain, but there is no record that he ever did. What is apparent is that by the beginning of the fourth century the church had spread widely and was beset by serious problems.

Scholars place the council some time between 300 and 309. Elvira assured its place in church history by being the first council whose canons have survived. The purpose of the council was disciplinary, to respond to a range of abuses which had arisen within the church. Nineteen bishops and 26 priests attended, although only the bishops signed the 81 canons which were enacted.

The tone of the canons was punitive. They provided harsh punishments for those guilty of idiolatry, divorce, incest, relations with pagans, Jews or heretics, usury and other matters — including the failure to observe clergy celibacy. Unfortunately, supporting records of the situations which gave rise to the need for such punitive canons and the theological and/or scriptural foundations upon which each canon rests are not available.

Of particular interest for present purposes is the following:

Canon 33
We decree that all bishops, priests and deacons in the service of the ministry are entirely

21

forbidden to have conjugal relations with their wives and to beget children; should anyone do so, let him be excluded from the honor of the clergy.[7]

A first reaction to this canon is shocked disbelief in light of the previously cited evidence of the acceptance of married clergy by Jesus and the early church. After one's initial reaction subsides, a radical question arises:

By what authority did the Council Fathers alter the established and honored practice of the first three centuries in the matter of free choice by individual clergy of the celibate or married state?

Since the facts of the situation are absent, the following conjecture is offered as one possible explanation of the environment within which the Council of Elvira might have taken place.

Might it have happened that, if not Paul himself, one of his many disciples introduced Christianity to Spain? And might that disciple have brought with him the apocalyptic ecclesiology and sexual moral theology of Paul? Is it conceivable that Christianity as first presented in Spain offered Paul's own celibate example as the ideal for all who would be true and total followers of Jesus? Most of all, was it taught that those who assumed the ministerial priesthood of Jesus should avoid the distractions of a wife and the "defilement" of the marital bed to preserve the purity needed for the cultic sacrifice of the Eucharist? Indeed, might marriage have been presented, not as a sacramental source of spousal sanctification and union with Jesus, but rather as an escape, a choice for the weak to quench the fire of the flesh?

To emphasize once again, the preceding questions are posed as conjecture, not as fact. However, if the reality is other than what has been conjectured, it becomes increasingly difficult to understand the actions of the Council Fathers who flaunted a 300-year tradition of free choice and presumed to establish a rigid norm of clerical celibacy which in years and centuries to come would be cited as basic teaching. To speak of a 300-year tradition of free choice does not imply that all priests chose to marry or to deny the existence of a celibate clergy from the earliest days. No conflict or predominance is supposed between married and celibate clergy. Rather, it is proposed that both married and celibate priests were accepted equally without prejudice prior to Elvira.

As already noted, history does not provide knowledge of the church's background in Spain preceding the council; the content of the council discussions; or, very importantly, the degree to which the canons were followed by priests and the faithful; or, if not followed, the manner in which the punishments set by the canons were imposed. There is no record, for instance, of how many married priests actually desisted from conjugal relations with their wives — a matter of some delicacy for episcopal authorities to investigate. Perhaps secondary evidence of noncompliance was available to bishops in those cases where the households of priests celebrated the birth of a new child a year or so after enactment of Canon 33. The simple truth is that we shall never know how well the canon was followed.

The absence of reliable and valid data on the implementing of the canons of Elvira is scarcely worth noting except that Canon 33 often is cited as a seminal example of early church discipline in the area of clergy celibacy. Given this fact, further reflection on the actual wording of the canon is appropriate.

First, the canon does not prohibit marriage by bishops, priests or deacons. Rather, it presumes that bishops, priests and deacons are married.

Second, the canon does not distinguish between marriage which was entered into prior to or after ordination.

Third, the canon focuses solely upon a restriction on conjugal relations and the procreation of children. It does not invalidate existing marriages, nor require the physical separation of clergy from their wives. In effect, it requires that clergy and their wives "live as brothers and sisters."

In light of the above, it is difficult not to conclude that Canon 33 violated the basic teaching of Jesus concerning marriage, namely, that what God has joined together no man — or council — should separate. Excluding the fine points of legal nuance, imposing upon a husband and wife joined in a valid sacramental union the requirement that they live under the same roof without the exercise of their conjugal rights constitutes a fundamental abrogation of spousal privilege and a severe form of de facto emotional and sexual separation. There is no evidence that the wives of priests in any way willingly surrendered their marital rights, including their rightful claims to the conjugal love of their husbands. One might dismiss the lack of consideration for the rights of wives as merely reflective of the cultural norms of the time; yet, injustice may not appeal to culture as a valid defense.

COUNCIL OF NICEA (325)

W hatever issues might be posed about Canon 33 of Elvira, the requirement of clergy celibacy took on a new dimension at the First Ecumenical Council of Nicea in 325. The council focused primarily upon the heresy of Arianism, but included among its actions the enactment of 20 canons relating to other matters, one of which pertained to clergy celibacy.

> ### Canon 3
> The great Synod has stringently forbidden any bishop, presbyter, deacon, or any one of the clergy whatever, to have a subintroducta dwelling with him, except only a mother, or sister, or aunt, or such persons only as are beyond all suspicion.[8]

As with Elvira, the canons of the council have survived intact but supporting statements upon which the canons were based have not come down to us. Reviewers of Canon 3 find difficulty in precisely interpreting the meaning of the term "subintroducta." It exceeds the scope of this consideration to dwell upon the term. Once more we find a law that is carried forward through the centuries without explanation of its rationale from the lawmakers.

While history has not provided documentation associated directly with either Elvira or Nicea to support the reasons for the imposition of mandatory celibacy, fourth and fifth century authorities such as Eusebius, St. Cyril of Jerusalem, St. Jerome and St. Epiphanius offer insights into the basis upon which the norm of celibacy was imposed.

Eusebius teaches that a priest who is engaged in ministry should observe continence and St. Cyril of Jerusalem urges priests who minister at the altar to remain aloof from women. St. Jerome says of priests who have wives that they cease to be husbands.[9] All of the reasons offered relate directly to the cultic responsibilities of the priest. Echoing Leviticus 15:18, these authorities regarded conjugal relations as a ritual defilement which rendered a priest unclean to offer the Eucharist.

Papal authority provided added weight to these interpretations, as in the instance of the remarks by Pope Leo (458-459) given below.

> Pope Leo expressed the norm in these words: ". . . in order for the union (of bishops, priests, and deacons) to change from carnal to spiritual, they must, without sending away their wives, live with them as if they did not have them, so that conjugal love be safeguarded and nuptial activity cease."[10]

Clearly the canons of church councils and the statements of respected early authorities are not to be ignored in considering the history of priestly marriage versus celibacy. However, there is more to consider.

COUNCIL OF TRULLO (692)

While the Church in the West moved steadily toward more stringent enforcement of clerical celibacy, the Church in the East did not follow a similar path. From earliest times the Church in the East honored the tradition of free choice and respected the Petrine example of married priesthood.

In 692 the Council of Trullo convened in Constantinople. Its name arose from the fact that it was held in the same domed hall as the Sixth Ecumenical Council (680-681). Since neither the fifth nor sixth general councils had included in their deliberations matters of discipline, the Council of Trullo sought to address these matters. Because of its purpose, to complete the work of the fifth and sixth general councils, it has earned the title of the Quinsext Council (i.e., the fifth-sixth council).

Despite the fact that the council considered itself to be an ecumenical council and was attended by 215 bishops (all of them Eastern), it is not counted as among the general councils of the church since the West was not really represented and because Pope Sergius (687-701) refused to accept the council decrees. However, one hundred years later Pope Hadrian I (772-795) recognized the Trullan decrees.

This council is worthy of consideration in some detail because of the respect given to it by the Eastern Churches and because of the significance of its canons which relate to the subject of this study. Among the 102 disciplinary canons of this council, three canons are cited for particular attention: canons 6, 13, 48. Canons 3 and 5 also are relevant.[11]

Canon 6

Since it is declared in the apostolic canons that of those who are advanced to the clergy unmarried, only lectors and cantors are able to marry; we also, maintaining this, determine that henceforth it is in nowise lawful for any subdeacon, deacon, or presbyter after his ordination to contract matrimony, but if he shall have dared to do so, let him be deposed. And if any of those who enter the clergy wishes to be joined to a wife in lawful marriage before he is ordained subdeacon, deacon, or presbyter, let it be done.

The canon is direct and to the point. Any single man who accepts the order of subdeacon, deacon, or priest must forever remain unmarried. Any attempt to marry after receiving orders is to be punished with removal or deposition from his office. However, anyone who wishes to marry before receiving subdiaconate, diaconate or priesthood should be allowed to do so.

Canon 13

Since we know it to be handed down as a rule of the Roman Church that those who are deemed worthy to be advanced to the diaconate or presbyterate should promise no longer to cohabit with their wives, we, preserving the ancient rule and apostolic perfection and order, will that the lawful marriages of men who are in holy orders be from this time forward firm, by no means dissolving their union with their wives nor depriving them of their mutual intercourse at a convenient time. Wherefore, if anyone shall have been found worthy to be ordained subdeacon, or deacon, or presbyter, he is by no means to be prohibited from admittance to such a rank, even if he shall live with a lawful wife. Nor shall it be demanded of him at the time of his ordination that he promise to abstain from lawful intercourse with his wife: lest we should affect injuriously marriage constituted by God and blessed by his presence, as the Gospel saith: "What God hath joined together let no man put asunder"; and the Apostle saith, "Marriage is honorable and the bed undefiled"; and again, "Art thou bound to a wife? Seek not to be loosed." But we know, as they who assembled at Carthage (with a care for the honest life of the clergy) said, that subdeacons, who handle the Holy Mysteries, and deacons, and presbyters should abstain from their consorts according to their own course [of ministration]. So that what has been handed down through the Apostles and preserved by ancient custom, we too likewise maintain, knowing that there is a time for all things and especially for fasting and prayer. For it is meet that they who assist at the divine altar should be absolutely continent when they are handling holy things, in order that they may be able to obtain from God what they ask in sincerity.

If therefore anyone shall have dared, contrary to the Apostolic Canons, to deprive any of those who are in holy orders, presbyter, or deacon, or subdeacon of cohabitation and intercourse with his lawful wife, let him be deposed. In like manner also if any presbyter or deacon on pretense of piety has dismissed his wife, let him be excluded from communion; and if he persevere in this let him be deposed.

This canon clearly recognizes and does not accept the rule of the Roman Church which forbids the cohabitation by priests with their wives. Declaring themselves more faithful than the Roman Church to the ancient rule, the Council Fathers strongly reaffirm the lawful right of priests to cohabit with their wives in full conjugal relationship. The scripture is cited as unassailable authority for the position of the council: "What God hath joined together let no man put asunder." The council imposed only one limitation on the conjugal rights of the clergy, namely, they directed that the clergy should abstain from having intercourse with their wives during the period when they were engaged in the exercise of their ministerial functions. This norm reflects the rules for cultic purity found in Leviticus.

Finally, the Council Fathers are not content simply to affirm a position which differs from the Roman Church. They reverse the person to be punished and decree that whoever dares to deprive any subdeacon, deacon or priest the right of cohabitation and marital intercourse with his lawful wife should be deposed.

Canon 48
The wife of him who is advanced to the Episcopal dignity shall be separated from her husband by their mutual consent, and after his ordination and consecration to the episcopate she shall enter a monastery situated at a distance from the abode of the bishop, and there let her enjoy the bishop's provision. And if she is deemed worthy she may be advanced to the dignity of a deaconess.

This canon requires the separation of husband and wife but only under unique and voluntary circumstances. Before a married man may be consecrated as a bishop, the canon requires that his wife be separated from him and enter a monastery. To this extent the canon imposes upon a prospective bishop a state of celibacy which is not required of clergy at the lower ranks. This rule, however, is far less harsh than the general rule of required celibacy found in the West.

The significant difference is the element of "mutual consent." Not only was it necessary for the married man to recognize and freely accept that as a consequence of his consecration as bishop he would be obliged to separate from his wife. It was necessary, as well, for the wife to agree to this separation. Without this "mutual consent" the consecration could not take place. It may be argued whether, in truth, either the man or his wife could exercise true freedom of choice in this situation. Nonetheless, this recognition of individual rights not only for the man but for his wife was remarkable and unique in canon law.

While the council fully supported the right of men to marry before ordination as a subdeacon, deacon, or priest, and the right to cohabitation and marital intercourse, the canons set limits as well.

Canon 3 prohibited from holy orders anyone who: married a second time; or married a widow, divorced woman, harlot, servant, or actress; or who had a concubine. Canon 5 mentions "persons free from suspicion" already identified in Canon 3 of Nicea.

Canon 5:
Let none of those who are on the priestly list possess any woman or maidservant, beyond

those who are enumerated in the canon as being persons free from suspicion, preserving himself hereby from being implicated in any blame. But if anyone transgresses our decree let him be deposed.

The 102 canons enacted at Trullo were sent to Pope Sergius for signature but he refused to accept them on the basis that they "lacked authority" and included "novel errors." Absent the papal signature, the canons were followed in the Eastern Church and about 100 years later were recognized by Pope Hadrian I. The canons of Trullo continue to the present time as the foundation of practice and canon law in the East.

The preceding review in some detail of what may be termed the "clergy canons" of the Council of Trullo provides the opportunity to consider a fundamental truth which rarely receives attention. People in general, including many Catholics, often use two distinctly different terms as synonyms while failing to consider a third important term. This inaccuracy at times may be of no great consequence, at other times the error may do a disservice or cause serious harm.

The two terms which mistakenly are often used interchangeably are: "Catholic Church" and "Roman Catholic Church." The third term which must be included is "Eastern Catholic Church." Some might say that it is a small question of semantics. The matter, however, is of greater significance as is amply shown by the above discussion of the canons from the Council of Trullo which differ basically on the subject of clergy marriage from the canons enacted by the Councils of Elvira and Nicea, and the instruction of Pope Leo the Great. The difference, of course, is disciplinary and not doctrinal in nature. But how can differences exist at so basic a level of discipline? Did the general rule of clergy celibacy change between Nicea and Trullo? That this is not the explanation will be seen shortly when the canons of later councils are considered. Then were the Council Fathers at Trullo in revolt against the Church? Again, this was not the case.

The truth, quite simply lies in the recognition of a distinction among the three terms mentioned above. There is only one, holy, catholic and apostolic Church. However, in different cultures and times there have always existed distinct manifestations of that Church in matters of liturgy and discipline. Within the Catholic church there exist two equally valid traditions , namely the Roman Catholic Church, also referred to as the Church of the West, and the Eastern Catholic Churches which consist of more than twenty distinct and valid traditions. While each of these separate traditions traces its origin to the early church, it is only since the *Decree On The Catholic Churches Of The Eastern Rite* of the Second Vatican Council that this long-neglected truth has entered the dialogue about the Church of the future. A fuller consideration of the Eastern Catholic traditions is presented in Chapter 3.

EFFORTS AT REFORM

In the centuries after Trullo, the Church in the West continued to emphasize with mixed results the rule of clergy celibacy. The role of the Church in secular matters, which began with the Edict of Milan, grew over time with the acquisition by the Church of increasingly large land holdings, great wealth, and broad power intermingled with the evils of lay investiture, simony, the transfer of properties and benefices from father to son, and varied other ills which infected the Church at all levels.

Enforcement of a rule of clergy celibacy for the priesthood in general was not facilitated by the fact that into the sixth and even the ninth centuries married popes ruled the Church. Pope Hormisdas (514-523) was married before ordination.[12] His son later became Pope Silverius (536-537). Three centuries later, Pope Adrian II (867-872), who is regarded as the last married pope, had at least one daughter.[13]

Pope Gregory VII (1073-1085), often referred to as Hildebrand, came to the papacy following the devastating Eastern Schism of 1054. Prior to his election as pope, Hildebrand, a Benedictine monk who had to be ordained a priest in order to accept the papacy, had a reputation as an able administrator of the Church's assets. An indication of the intimate relationship which existed at the time between religious and secular power is seen in the fact that Gregory did not proceed with the ceremony of his consecration until he received concurrence from Emperor Henry IV of Germany.

As soon as he became pope, Gregory energetically introduced an extensive policy of reform and renewal within the Church. In particular, he identified simony and clerical incontinence as the two root causes of the deplorable condition of the Church at the time.

In 1074 he issued decrees which demanded that clerics who had paid to obtain their positions should be removed from the ministry, that the purchase or sale of ecclesiastical rights should be prohibited, that incontinent clerics should cease to exercise the sacred ministry, and that the faithful should refuse to accept the ministration of any clerics who disobeyed Gregory's directives.

The orders of Gregory were met in many instances by indifferent bishops and indignant priests. Reportedly, at Nuremberg the married priests informed the papal legate that they would rather renounce their priesthood than their wives, and that he (Gregory) for whom men were not good enough might go seek angels to preside over the Churches.[14]

Gregory persisted in his commitment to reform but was distracted by an ongoing conflict with Henry IV regarding the improper appointment of prelates by the German emperor. In the end both Gregory and Henry fell victims to their enemies. Gregory withdrew from Rome and spent his last year before death at Monte Cassino.

As the eleventh century came to an end, the Church was in a general state of disorder: the disastrous rupture with the East endured, the widespread evil of simony persisted, and the unrestrained practices of marriage and concubinage among the clergy continued despite repeated condemnations by papal decrees and canons of councils. A breakthrough on the issue of simony, or lay investiture, came in 1122 when Pope Callistus II and Emperor Henry V signed the Concordat of Worms. This first formal agreement between the papacy and a civil power established a distinction between the spiritual power of the papacy, signified by the ring and crosier, and the temporal power of the emperor, signified by the scepter. It provided acceptance by the emperor that spiritual jurisdiction could be granted solely by the Church. For the Church's part, the pope conceded to the emperor the right to be present at the election of bishops and abbots and to have a role in resolving contested elections.

FREDERICK J. LUHMANN

THE LATERAN COUNCILS

$\mathbb{T}$o mark the importance of the concordat, Callistus convened the first general council to be held in the West, the gathering known in history as the First Lateran Council of 1123[15]. As with many councils, no copy of the overall actions of the council exists but an incomplete list of the council's canons has survived over time. The following two canons are significant to this study.

Canon 3
We absolutely forbid priests, deacons, and subdeacons to associate with concubines and women, or to live with women other than such as the Nicene Council (canon 3) for reasons of necessity permitted, namely, the mother, sister, or aunt, or any such person concerning whom no suspicion could arise.

This canon does little other than to repeat the official position of the Church which was first articulated by the Council of Nicea. The wording is slightly different but substantially identical with the policy stated 800 years earlier.

Canon 21
We absolutely forbid priests, deacons, subdeacons and monks to have concubines or to contract marriage. We decree in accordance with the definitions of the sacred canons, that marriages already contracted by such persons must be dissolved, and the persons be condemned to do penance.

Clearly the Council Fathers wanted to leave no doubt about their feelings on the subjects of concubines and marriage. Beyond being merely repetitive of Canon 3, this canon offers several additional points to consider.

The canon forbids clergy to marry (a future action). As for marriages already contracted they must be dissolved. The unavoidable conclusion is that the Council Fathers recognized the existing marriages of clergy as being valid, albeit illicit. Indeed, if the marriages were not valid, there would have been no need to distinguish between such marriages and concubinage. A priest who lived with a woman in an invalid union, by definition, would have been guilty of concubinage. The canon does not cite the means or the authority by which a valid marriage is to be dissolved, nor explain how the command to dissolve a valid marriage does not violate the scriptural command: "What God has joined let no man separate."

The year following the council Callistus II died and was succeeded by Honorius II (1124-1130) who in turn was followed by Innocent II (1130-1143).

The election of Innocent immediately precipitated the Church into turmoil because of the appearance of Pope Anacletus II, the antipope, who gained a large following among the faithful and powerful lords. Eight years of conflict followed before Innocent gained undisputed title to the papacy when Anacletus II died in 1138.

In order to bring unity after the years of schism by the followers of Anacletus, Innocent convened the Second Lateran Council of 1139.[16] The council decreed 30 canons to restore order and correct abuses which were prevalent in the Church. While the canons remain, as with many other councils, no other records are available.   For present considerations two of the canons are important.

Canon 6
We also decree that those who in the subdiaconate and higher orders have contracted marriage or have concubines, be deprived of their office and ecclesiastical benefice. For since they should be and are called the temple of God, the vessel of the Lord, the abode of the Holy Spirit, it is unbecoming that they indulge in marriage and in impurities.

It appears from the tone of this canon that, 16 years after Canon 21 of the First Lateran Council decreed that marriages of priests, deacons, subdeacons and monks be dissolved, little had changed.   Therefore, in this canon Lateran II goes beyond the general directive of Canon 21 that offenders be "condemned to do penance" and imposes specific and very severe punishments. Henceforth, any clergy who continue to live in marriage or concubinage are to be deprived of their offices and ecclesiastical benefices.

The final words of the canon provide an insight into the mind of the Council Fathers. They express the view that, since marriage is a form of "indulgence," clergy in higher orders should keep themselves from such unbecoming behavior. Clergy are reminded that theirs is a higher calling: to be temples of God, vessels of the Lord, abodes of the Holy Spirit. And what of the laity? Nothing is said. One is left to draw the obvious conclusion that they are not called to such spiritual intimacies.

In the next canon the Council Fathers raised the stakes even higher. Having been unable to coerce the clergy into compliance directly, they attacked the issue from another direction. They turned to the laity in the hope of cutting off the base of support of recalcitrant clergy.

> Canon 7
> Following in the footsteps of our predecessors, the Roman pontiffs Gregory VII, Urban, and Paschal, we command that no one attend the masses of those who are known to have wives or concubines. But that the law of continence and purity, so pleasing to God, may become more general among persons constituted in sacred orders, we decree that bishops, priests, deacons, subdeacons, canons regular, monks, and professed clerics who, transgressing the holy precept, have dared to contract marriage, shall be separated. For a union of this kind which has been contracted in violation of the ecclesiastical law, we do not regard as matrimony. Those who have been separated from each other shall do penance commensurate with such excesses.

The new strategy employed to put an end to the prevalence of married clergy was to command the faithful not to attend masses of those clergy who were known to have either wives or concubines. The fact that previous commands directed at the clergy to a large extent had not been heeded is clear from the stated purpose of the command, namely to bring about more general observance of the law of continence.

Further, the Council Fathers stated ". . . we do not regard as matrimony . . . " the marriages of clergy contracted in violation of ecclesiastical law. In effect, the council decreed that an action which previously had been regarded as "illicit but valid" became "both illicit and invalid." The council determined that because of church law clergy in higher orders had no capacity to enter into a valid marriage, and any attempted union was null and void from its inception. The canon does not provide any theological or scriptural basis for this radical change in the law, nor does the canon acknowledge the continued acceptance of married priests in the Eastern Churches.

COUNCIL OF TRENT (1545-1563)

Following the Second Lateran Council, over 400 years passed before the Church assembled in the landmark Council of Trent (1545-1563.) In the aftermath of the Protestant Reformation, the council confronted an extensive and radical agenda focused upon major reform of varied and deep-rooted abuses which afflicted the Church. The scope and controversial nature of the issues before the council were of such nature that it was not possible to address all matters in one continuous gathering. As a result, the council met in a long-running series of sessions which convened at various locations between December 13, 1545 and December 4, 1563.

At the Twenty-Third Session[17] of the council held in July 1563 a number of decrees were issued concerning clerical orders.

Chapter XII prescribed minimum ages for receipt of major orders: subdeacon, 22; deacon, 23; priesthood, 25. Bishops were admonished that only the worthy who evidenced a commendable life were to be ordained.

Chapter XIV directed that anyone who was to be raised to the priesthood must have served in the office of deacon for an entire year, have been approved by a careful examination as capable of teaching people the things necessary for salvation, be fit to administer the sacraments, and be a conspicuous example of piety, chasteness, and good morals.

An exception was made to allow the time between becoming a deacon and ordination to priesthood to be shortened when in the judgement of the bishop it was appropriate "for the utility and necessity of the Church."

On November 11, 1563, The Twenty- Fourth Session[18] of the council focused on the sacrament of matrimony.

Although the introduction of a discussion of the council's canons on marriage may appear to be a digression, it is directly related to this study. Several canons are presented below with comments following the last.

Canon 1
If anyone saith, that matrimony is not truly and properly one of the seven sacraments of the evangelic law (a sacrament) instituted by Christ the Lord; but that it has been invented by men in the Church; and that it does not confer grace; let him be anathema.

Canon 9
If anyone saith, that clerics constituted in sacred orders, or regulars, who have solemnly professed chastity, are able to contract marriage, and that being contracted it is valid, notwithstanding the ecclesiastical law, or vow; and that the contrary is no thing else than to condemn marriage; and, that all who do not feel that they have the gift of chastity, even though they have made a vow thereof, may contract marriage; let him be anathema; seeing that God refuses not that gift to those who ask for it rightly, neither does He suffer us to be tempted above that which we are able.

Canon 10
If anyone saith, that the marriage state is to be placed above the state of virginity, or of celibacy, and that it is not better and more blessed to remain in virginity, or in celibacy, than to be united in matrimony, let him be anathema.

Canon 1 is remarkable in that it took the Church almost 1600 years to affirm in this solemn manner so basic and obvious a matter of doctrine as this: Matrimony is one of the seven sacraments and it confers grace. One wonders what had been the catechesis about matrimony over the centuries?

Canon 9 contains in one lengthy sentence several decrees which represent present day teaching.

1. Clerics in sacred orders or professed regulars are unable to contract a valid marriage because it is forbidden, either because of ecclesiastical law alone or, in the case of professed regulars, because of the vow of chastity which they have taken.

2. Neither clerics in sacred orders nor professed regulars who have taken the vow of chastity are able to marry because they feel that they do not have the gift of chastity.

3. God does not allow us to be tempted above what we are able.

4. If anyone does not accept these decrees, let him be anathema.

The terms of the discussion have not progressed much over the centuries.

Canon 10 is directed at stemming the sentiment spread by Protestant Reformers of the era who dispensed with the requirement for celibacy of the clergy.

In their zeal to protect celibacy, the Council Fathers took things too far. Rather than simply extol the merits of the celibate life, they felt compelled to denigrate marriage in the process. They not only condemn those who put marriage above celibacy, but they espouse the opposite and equally untenable position: the belief that celibacy per se is superior to marriage.

SECOND VATICAN COUNCIL

$\mathbb{V}$atican II (1962-1965) was the twenty-first Ecumenical Council of the Catholic Church. Over 1600 years had intervened since the Council of Nicea, 400 years since the Council of Trent. As the Council opened on October 12, 1962, the agenda at hand was to clothe the Church with the garments of spiritual renewal which Pope John XXIII had envisioned when he first called the Church to assemble over three years earlier.

Of the 16 documents produced by the council, two are considered here:

Decree On The Catholic Churches Of The Eastern Rite (November 21, 1964)[19] and **Decree On The Ministry And Life Of Priests** (December 7, 1965).[20]

I. DECREE ON THE CATHOLIC CHURCHES OF THE EASTERN RITE

Preamble
1. The Catholic Church holds in high esteem the institutions, liturgical rites, ecclesiastical traditions and the established standards of the Christian life of the Eastern Churches, for in them, distinguished as they are for their venerable antiquity, there remains conspicuous the tradition that has been handed down from the Apostles through the Fathers and that forms part of the divinely revealed and undivided heritage of the universal Church.

These opening lines of the decree express the highest respect for the institutions, liturgical rites, traditions and standards of the Eastern Churches which are acknowledged to be of great antiquity and to have descended from the Apostles. Of great significance is the recognition that the traditions and practices of the Eastern Churches constitute a part of the divinely revealed and undivided heritage of the universal Church. As such, it is distressing that previous councils included so little — if any — consideration of the life of the Eastern Churches in legislating for the universal Church. Select excerpts of the decree are considered below.

Preservation of the Spiritual Heritage of the Eastern Churches

5. History, tradition and abundant ecclesiastical institutions bear outstanding witness to the great merit owing to the Eastern Churches by the universal Church. The Sacred Council, therefore, not only accords to this ecclesiastical and spiritual heritage the high regard which is its due and rightful praise, but also unhesitatingly looks on it as the heritage of the universal Church. For this reason it solemnly declares that the Churches of the East, as much as those of the West, have a full right and are in duty bound to rule themselves, each in accordance with its own established disciplines, since all these are praiseworthy by reason of their venerable antiquity, more harmonious with the character of their faithful and more suited to the promotion of the good of souls.

Once more in this paragraph the council recognized the debt of praise that the universal Church owes to the

Eastern Churches and embraced the ecclesiastical and spiritual heritage of the East as that of the universal Church.

In light of this high regard, the council declared that the Churches of the East, as much as those of the West, not only have a full right but are duty bound to rule themselves according to their own established disciplines. Why is this so? Because they are of ancient origin and very importantly, are more harmonious with the character of their faithful, and more suited to the promotion of the good of souls. These two criteria might well serve as the "litmus test" for each rule of discipline throughout the Church.

The Discipline of the Sacraments

12. The Sacred Ecumenical Council confirms and approves the ancient discipline of the sacraments existing in the Oriental Churches, as also the ritual practices connected with their celebration and administration and ardently desires that this should be reestablished if circumstances warrant it.

This approval of the sacramental practices of the Eastern Churches does not provide specifics. Subsequent paragraphs consider confirmation, confession, marriage and Sunday observance. Comments about the Sacrament of Orders are contained in Paragraph 17.

17. In order that the ancient established practice of the Sacrament of Orders in the Eastern Churches may flourish again, this Sacred Council ardently desires that the office of permanent diaconate should, where it has fallen into disuse, be restored. The legislative authorities of each individual church should

decide about the subdiaconate and the minor orders and the rights and obligations that attach to them.

Each of the clerical orders is mentioned except for the priesthood. A sincere concern by the council to assure that the Sacrament of Orders flourishes in the East could not by oversight have failed to address the priesthood as the highest of the orders. While the council previously expressed approval for the existing discipline of the sacraments in the Eastern Churches, it could not bring itself explicitly to praise the discipline of a married priesthood.

II. DECREE ON THE MINISTRY AND LIFE OF PRIESTS

This lengthy decree is divided into three chapters and 22 numbered topics. The present discussion focuses upon Chapter III The Life of Priests, Section 2, Special Spiritual Requirements in the Life of a Priest, numbers 16 and 17.

16. (Celibacy is to be embraced and esteemed as a gift)
Perfect and perpetual continence for the sake of the Kingdom of Heaven, commended by Christ the Lord and through the course of time as well as in our own days freely accepted and observed in a praiseworthy manner by many of the faithful, is held by the Church to be of great value in a special manner for the priestly life. It is at the same time a sign and a stimulus for pastoral charity and a special source of spiritual fecundity in the world. Indeed, it is not demanded by the very nature of the priesthood, as is apparent from the practice of the early

Church and from the traditions of the Eastern Churches, where, besides those who with all the bishops, by a gift of grace, choose to observe celibacy, there are also married priests of highest merit. Let this holy synod, while it commends ecclesiastical celibacy, in no way intend to alter that different discipline which legitimately flourishes in the Eastern Churches. It permanently exhorts all those who have received the priesthood in marriage to persevere in their holy vocation so that they may fully and generously continue to expend themselves for the sake of the flock commended to them.

Indeed celibacy has a many faceted suitability for the priesthood. For the whole priestly mission is dedicated to the service of a new humanity which Christ, the victor over death, has aroused through His Spirit in the world and which has its origin "not of blood, nor of the will of the flesh, nor of the will of man but of God" (John 1:13). Through virginity, then, or celibacy observed for the Kingdom of Heaven, priests are consecrated to Christ by a new and exceptional reason. They adhere to Him more easily with an undivided heart, they dedicate themselves more freely in Him and through Him to the service of God and men, and they more expeditiously minister to His Kingdom and the work of heavenly regeneration, and thus they are apt to accept, in a broad sense, paternity in Christ. In this way they profess themselves before men as willing to be dedicated to the office committed to them—namely, to commit themselves faithfully to one man and to show themselves as a chaste virgin for Christ and thus to evoke the mysterious marriage established by Christ, and fully to be manifested in the future, in which the Church has Christ as her only Spouse. They give, moreover, a living sign of the world to come, by a faith and charity already made present, in which the children of the resurrection neither marry nor take wives.

For these reasons, based on the mystery of Christ and His mission, celibacy, which first was recommended to priests, later in the Latin Church was imposed upon all who were to be promoted to sacred orders. This legislation, pertaining to those who are destined for the priesthood, this holy synod again approves and confirms, fully trusting this gift of the Spirit so fitting for the priesthood of Christ through the Sacrament of Orders—and also the whole Church—humbly and fervently pray for it. This sacred synod also exhorts all priests who, in following the example of Christ freely receive sacred celibacy as a grace of God, that they magnanimously and wholeheartedly adhere to it, and that persevering faithful in it, they may acknowledge this outstanding gift of the Father which is so openly praised and extolled by the Lord. Let them keep before their eyes the great mysteries signified by it and fulfilled in it. Insofar as perfect continence is thought by many men to be impossible in our times, to that extent priests should all the more humbly and steadfastly pray with the Church for that grace of fidelity, which is never denied those who seek it, and use all the supernatural and natural aids available. They should seek, lest they omit them, the ascetical norms which have been proved by the experience of the Church and which are scarcely less necessary in the contemporary world. This holy synod asks not only priests but all the faithful that they might receive this precious gift of priestly celibacy in their hearts and ask of God that He will always bestow this gift upon His Church.

17. (Relationship to the world and temporal goods, and voluntary poverty.)
Priests, moreover, are invited to embrace voluntary poverty by which they are more manifestly conformed to Christ and become eager in the sacred ministry. For Christ, though He was rich, became poor on account of us, that by His need we might become rich. And by their example the apostles witnessed that a free gift of God is to be freely given, with the knowledge of how to sustain both abundance and need. A certain common use of goods, similar to the common possession of goods in the history of the primitive Church, furnishes an excellent means of pastoral charity. By living this form of life, priests can laudably reduce to practice that spirit of poverty commended by Christ.

Led by the Spirit of the Lord, who anointed the Savior and sent Him to evangelize the poor, priests, therefore, and also bishops, should avoid everything which in any way could turn the poor away. Before the other followers of Christ, let priests set aside every appearance of vanity in their possessions. Let them arrange their homes so that they might not appear unapproachable to anyone, lest anyone, even the most humble, fear to visit them.

The *Decree on the Ministry and Life of Priests* clearly teaches that celibacy is not demanded by the very nature of the priesthood. It further acknowledges that celibacy was not required in the early Church nor is it required to the present day in the Eastern Churches. What the decree fails to do is to provide a clear understanding as to why, after 300 years of optional celibacy, the Council of Nicea and subsequent councils withdrew in the Western Church the freedom which clergy enjoyed from apostolic times to elect between marriage and celibacy, and replaced that freedom with a rule of mandatory celibacy. The decree takes a small step to acknowledge married priests in the Eastern Churches and to exhort them to persevere in their holy vocation (that is, priesthood, not marriage.) However, at no place in the decree is the compatibility of priesthood and marriage affirmed, nor is there any acknowledgment of spiritual benefits to priestly ministry which may flow from the mutually interactive graces of two sacraments, marriage and priestly ordination.

Having acknowledged the general acceptance of married clergy throughout the early Church and the continuity of a married priesthood in the East, the decree largely dismisses these two facts without further comment and proceeds to extol the ideal of celibacy for the priesthood. Celibacy, the decree states, is of special value to the priestly life, has a many faceted suitability for the priesthood, provides priests with a new and exceptional consecration to Christ, permits priests to adhere to Christ more easily with an undivided heart, and to dedicate themselves more freely to the service of God and men. At one and the same time, celibate priests, it is stated, accept in a broad sense paternity in Christ and show themselves as chaste virgins for Christ. The mixed metaphor in the description goes unnoticed.

It is of interest that the decree places great emphasis upon the reasonable nature of the mandate to priestly celibacy based upon the necessity for the priest to model Christ's virginity, while priests are only encouraged to "voluntary poverty" to follow Christ who had no place to lay his head.

The language in support of the special value of celibacy for the priestly life draws heavily upon the concepts and wording of 1Cor 7:1-9 and 32-35. (Observations offered at pp. 13-14 on these texts apply equally to this part of the decree.)

TODAY

Chapter 3

1. PASTORAL PROVISIONS

 $\mathbb{D}$ iscussions about many areas of Church life often note a convenient, if simplistic, division between pre-Vatican II and post-Vatican II rules, situations, circumstances, or thinking. The present topic is not one which easily lends itself to this approach. In the consideration of marriage—celibacy—priesthood, the preceding chapters have shown that in the history of the Church there never existed a time when either all priests were married or all priests were celibate.

What has been documented is that in apostolic times and in the first three centuries of the Church all priests were free to choose marriage or celibacy based upon the particular charism which each received. Beginning in the fourth century, and continuing over many succeeding centuries, laws were introduced and coercive methods applied to restrict the freedom of choice for priests of the Western Church. However, it was not until the twelfth century that the Second Lateran Council decreed that clergy in major orders were incapable of entering into a valid marriage.

While the Council does not address the point, it is clear that ordination to major orders became an impediment to marriage **solely** for clergy bound by the canon law of the Church in the West. Both prior to and after the Second Lateran Council, priests in the East, where canon law on this matter is founded on the Council of Trullo, were recognized as having the freedom to choose either celibacy or marriage before receiving major orders.

The *Decree on the Ministry and Life of Priests* promulgated by Vatican II served to reiterate the Church's firm commitment to the ideal of priestly celibacy *as most suitable for the priesthood*, this despite the unbroken tradition of the Eastern Catholic Churches which have maintained the freedom of choice received from the early Church. One wonders how all of the married priests of the Eastern Churches received the thinly veiled implication of the Decree that their married priesthood denied to them the bounty of special graces and efficacious ministry which the Council recognized as uniquely available to celibate priests.

Priesthood in the Eastern Churches will receive separate consideration. First, it is important to focus upon a number of situations during the last 50 years in which the Holy See has granted exceptions in the Western Church to the strict and universal rule of priestly celibacy.

Fichter[21] and Hill[22] both report that Pope Pius XII permitted several exceptions to the rule of celibacy. Fichter writes that Pope Pius XII demonstrated a willingness to accept married priests in several cases. In 1951 he granted an indult to Bishop Alberto Stohr of Mainz, Germany in favor of Rudolf Goethe, a married Lutheran pastor who was ordained as a Catholic priest on his seventy-first birthday. Two younger ministers, Eugen Scheytt and Otto Melchers were ordained the following year. Then in 1953 another married convert, Martin Giebner, was ordained as the fourth married priest in Germany. Again, in 1964, Ernest Beck, a married Lutheran minister was ordained by the Archbishop of Mainz. Hill provides the information that married pastors of the Reformed Church in Germany were received, together with their congregations, into full communion with Rome and that the married pastors were ordained as Catholic priests in order to minister to their congregations. Hill adds that there is no published information regarding any similar cases during the pontificates of John XXIII, Paul VI or John Paul I.

The next significant public document on this subject was Paul VI's encyclical, *Sacerdotalis caelibatus* which was issued in 1967, just two years after the end of Vatican II and the issuance of the *Decree on the Ministry and Life of Priests*. Paul VI apparently felt the need to expand upon the discussion of "priestly celibacy" found in the decree. However, while he extolled the intimate connection and value of celibacy to the priesthood, Paul VI provided an opening for the reintroduction some years later of a married priesthood into the Western Church.

Pope Paul VI writes in numbers 42-43 of the encyclical:

> 42. In virtue of the fundamental norm of the government of the Catholic Church, to which We alluded above, while on the one hand, the law requiring a freely chosen and perpetual celibacy of those who are admitted to Holy Orders remains unchanged, on the other hand,

a study may be allowed of the particular circumstances of married sacred ministers of Churches of other Christian communities separated from the Catholic communion, and of the possibility of admitting to priestly functions those who desire to adhere to the fullness of this communion and to continue to exercise the sacred ministry. The circumstances must be such, however, as not to prejudice the existing discipline regarding celibacy.

43. All this, however, does not signify a relaxation of the existing law, and must not be interpreted as a prelude to its abolition. There are better things to do than to promote this hypothesis, which tears down that vigor and love in which celibacy finds security and happiness, and which obscures the true doctrine that justifies its existence and exalts its splendor. It would be much better to promote serious studies in defense of the spiritual meaning and moral value of virginity and celibacy.

In reading Paul's words, the image comes to mind of opening the barn door just a little bit. Whatever Paul's intent, the study to which he referred never seems to have been undertaken. However, in less than a decade, events which occurred in another Christian church initiated a process which would open the priesthood of the Catholic Church in the West to a particular category of married men.

UNITED STATES

During the 1970's the Episcopal Church in the United States experienced a number of changes in areas of moral teaching, liturgical life, and disciplinary practice which some members believed altered the nature of the Church to an unacceptable degree. Those who were most uncomfortable with the changes included members frequently described as "high-church" Episcopalians or Anglo-Catholic "Papalists" who held high hopes of ultimate reunion with the Catholic Church. These members increasingly distanced themselves from a number of positions which the Episcopal Church adopted. This group also was distressed by the introduction in 1973 of a revised *Book of Common Prayer* which replaced their much-loved 1928 version of the Book. For some, the ultimate rupture of allegiance came when the Episcopal Church allowed the ordination of women priests.

The first effort in the Episcopal Church to allow women to be ordained as priests and bishops was the introduction of a motion at the 1970 General Convention of the Church.[23] The motion was defeated but showed a surprising degree of support. Organized efforts to promote the ordination of women came into existence following the convention. Once again, a motion was introduced at the 1973 Convention in Louisville, Kentucky. The motion again met defeat but the issue was not put to rest.

Within a year, a group of supporters organized and accomplished the "extraordinary" ordination to the priesthood of 11 women. The ordinations were performed in Philadelphia on July 29, 1974, by three legally consecrated

Episcopal bishops. On September 7, 1975, four additional women were ordained in Washington, D.C., by a retired Episcopal bishop. All of the "extraordinary" ordinations were judged to be invalid by the House of Bishops of the Church. Nonetheless, the House of Bishops at a meeting later that same year voted support for the ordination of women as both priests and bishops.

Finally, at the 1976 General Convention in Minneapolis the Episcopal Church accepted the ordination of women. A resolution passed which stated that canon law should provide equal applicability to men and women for ordination to the orders of bishops, priests and deacons. The sense of this resolution is incorporated in present canon law as indicated below.

1997 Constitution and Canons of the Episcopal Church

TITLE III. CANON 4: OF POSTULANTS FOR HOLY ORDERS

Sec. 1 All Bishops of Dioceses and other Clergy shall make provisions to identify fit persons for Holy Orders and encourage them to present themselves for Postulancy. No one shall be denied access to the selection process for ordination in this Church because of race, color, ethnic origin, sex, national origin, marital status, sexual orientation, disabilities or age, except as otherwise specified by these Canons. No right to ordination is hereby established.[24]

As "high-church" members of the Episcopal Church distanced themselves from decisions and actions of their Church which they believed lessened the possibility of ultimate reunification with the Catholic Church, some of their number began a journey toward Rome.

In 1976 a group of "high-church" Episcopalians met under the leadership of members of the Anglican Society of the Holy Cross. The society was committed to ecumenical activities with the goal of reunification with the Catholic Church. The group concluded that the Episcopal Church was moving away from traditional beliefs and practices of the Anglican heritage and that direct initiatives to accomplish reunification with the Catholic Church were necessary.

Following the Minneapolis Convention, some individuals and congregations separated from the Episcopal Church. One such group was the Pro-Diocese of St. Augustine of Canterbury.[25] The Pro-Diocese consisted of several congregations which hoped to attain a Uniate status within the Catholic Church in which they would be able to retain a common Anglican identity with their own bishop, liturgy and culture.

Representatives of the Pro-Diocese met in Rome with Cardinal Franjo Seper, Prefect of the Congregation for the Doctrine of the Faith. The initial meeting led to further contact and another meeting in 1979. The proposal of the Pro-Diocese for acceptance as a separate Uniate Rite was not well received in Rome. However, over time an alternative was developed that involved the concept of a "unit of common identity" but which did not enjoy separate Uniate status. This proposal became known as the Seper compromise.

The Pro-Diocese had circumvented the Bishops of the United States and had taken its case directly to Rome. This approach did not prove successful and in time the Pro-Diocese disbanded. Others who were equally disaffected with the direction of the Episcopal Church proceeded along more accepted channels of communication. In the spring of 1977 Father James Parker and Father Lawrence Lossing, who also were members of the Anglican Society of the Holy Cross, brought their request for acceptance by the Catholic Church to the Apostolic Delegate, Archbishop Jean Jadot. The Apostolic Delegate agreed to transmit their request to Archbishop John Quinn, President of the National Conference of Catholic Bishops, and to take their request to Rome personally.

> Fichter offers the following observation:
> Since the implementation of any Uniate program of this size would ultimately require the cooperation of bishops at the diocesan level, the Seper compromise was thoroughly discussed at two meetings of the National Conference of Catholic Bishops. In May 1979, the Bishops passed a resolution requesting that the Holy See allow married Episcopal priests to enter the Catholic priesthood, with a provision that some groups would be permitted to preserve their common Anglican identity. The vote was not unanimous. Some bishops did not want the bother of accommodating "common identity" parishes in their dioceses. A more vehement opposition came from Eastern-rite Bishops who complained that the 1929 decree, *Cum data fuerit,* had eliminated married Byzantine clergy from the United States. Why should American bishops now make an exception for convert Anglicans?[26]

More than a year passed before the Congregation for the Doctrine of the Faith replied to the request of the National Conference of Catholic Bishops in a letter to Archbishop John R. Quinn which is reproduced on the following pages.

July 22, 1980
Prot. N. 66/77

His Excellency, Most Reverend John R. Quinn
Archbishop of San Francisco
President, N.C.C.B.

Your Excellency,

The Congregation for the Doctrine of the
Faith, in its Ordinary Session of June 18, 1980,
has taken the following decision in regard to
the Episcopalians who seek reconciliation with
and entrance into the Catholic Church.

I. General Decisions:

1) The admission of these persons, even in a
group, should be considered the reconciliation
of individual persons, as described in the
Decree on Ecumenism *Redintegratio Unitatis*,
n. 4, of the Second Vatican Council.

2) It will be appropriate to formulate a statute
or "pastoral provision" which provides for a
"common identity" for the group.

II. Elements of the "Common Identity":

1) Structures: the preference expressed by the
majority of the Episcopal Conference for the
insertion of these reconciled Episcopalians into
the diocesan structures under the jurisdiction of
the local Ordinaries is recognized.
Nevertheless, the possibility of some other type

of structure as provided for by canonical dispositions, and as suited to the needs of the group, is not excluded.

2) Liturgy: The group may retain certain elements of the Anglican liturgy; these are to be determined by a Commission of the Congregation set up for this purpose. Use of these elements will be reserved to the former members of the Anglican Communion. Should a former Anglican priest celebrate public liturgy outside this group, he will be required to adopt the common Roman Rite.

3) Discipline: (a) To married Episcopalian priests who may be ordained Catholic priests, the following stipulations will apply: they may not become bishops; and they may not remarry in case of widowhood. (b) Future candidates for the priesthood must follow the discipline of celibacy. (c) Special care must be taken on the pastoral level to avoid any misunderstanding regarding the Church's discipline of celibacy.

III. Steps required for admission to full communion:

1) Theological-catechetical preparation is to be provided according to need.

2) A profession of faith (with appropriate additions to address the points on which there is divergence of teaching between the Anglican Communion and the Catholic Church) is to be made personally by all (ministers and faithful) as a *conditio sine qua non.*

3) Reordination of the Episcopalian clergy, even those who are married, shall be allowed in accord with the customary practice, after the examination of each individual case by the Congregation for the Doctrine of the Faith.

IV. The statute or "pastoral provision" will not be definitive, but rather will be granted *ad tempus non determinatum*.

V. Particulars regarding the execution of the decision:

1) The contents of the statute or "pastoral provision" are to be determined with the agreement of the Episcopal Conference. In what concerns the liturgical aspects of the statute, the Congregation for the Sacraments and Divine Worship will be asked for its accord. The Congregation for the Doctrine of the Faith will keep informed of any developments both the Secretariat for Promoting Christian Unity and the Congregation for the Oriental Churches (the latter in view of the possible influence on the particular dispositions for ecclesiastical celibacy among Eastern-rite priests in the United States).

2) A Catholic Ecclesiastical Delegate, preferably a Bishop, should be designated, with the approval of the Episcopal Conference, as the responsible person to oversee the practical application of the decisions here reported and to deal with the Congregation for the Doctrine of the Faith in what pertains to this question.

3) These decisions should be implemented with all deliberate speed in view of the waiting period already undergone by the Episcopalians who have presented this request.

These decisions were approved by His Holiness Pope John Paul II in the audience granted to the undersigned Cardinal Prefect of the Congregation on June 20, 1980.

The complexity of the above decisions, Your Excellency, recommends early contact between yourself and the Congregation in order to discuss the details and procedures for their implementation. Given your knowledge of the matter, it would seem ideal that, even after your term as President of the Episcopal Conference has expired, you might remain as Bishop Delegate (cf. V, 2) responsible for overseeing the admission of these persons into full communion with the Catholic Church. Permit me to express the hope that, if convenient for you, you will contact the Congregation for the purpose of initiating the necessary discussion of this question during your stay in Rome to participate in the 1980 Synod of Bishops.

Finally, I am enclosing a letter which I would be grateful to you for forwarding, after you have taken note of its contents, to Father John Barker of the Pro-Diocese of St. Augustine of Canterbury, informing him that their petition has been accepted in principle. Since you will be in the best position to know what publicity may be deemed unavoidable or suitable, I would like to leave in your hands the manner and timing of any communication about the fact or nature of the decisions here reported. I am sure you will have already noted in the decisions as reported a concern for the sensitive areas of ecumenism and celibacy.

You will no doubt want to inform Bishops Law and Lessing of the abovementioned decisions, since they were so closely involved in the negotiations during various phases. Since the group in question involves a certain number of English clergy and faithful, The Congregation will undertake to give the necessary information to the hierarchy of England and Wales.

With every best wish for Your Excellency, I remain

Sincerely yours in Christ,

/S/ Franjo Card. Seper, Pref.

Cardinal Seper's letter in a dry, low-key tone granted an exception to the disciplinary principle of absolute priestly celibacy which the Church in the West had sought to enforce, not always with complete success, since the fourth century. A small number of Episcopal priests (much fewer than 50) had accomplished a change in the practice, if not in the written law, of the Church. The Episcopal priests, of course, did not directly change the practice. Rather, they presented the occasion for change by requesting reconciliation with the Catholic Church and by asking for priestly ordination while being permitted to continue their married lives. The National Conference of Catholic Bishops, for its part, in response to the initiative of the Episcopalian priests, passed a supporting resolution and forwarded the resolution to the Holy See.

The carefully worded Seper letter informed the Bishops' Conference of approval by the Holy See of the resolution and outlined the framework for implementing a process by which married Episcopal priests, together with their wives and children, could be accepted into the Church and be eligible for ordination as Catholic priests.

The introduction of the Seper letter states immediately that the decision to approve the request of the Bishops' Conference was made by the Congregation for the Doctrine of the Faith (CDF). Only later were the decisions of the CDF approved by Pope John Paul II. The central role of the CDF in the initial decisions and in subsequent matters of implementation is clearly evident here and elsewhere in the letter. The letter goes on to indicate that much still remains to be done before the principles outlined in the letter can be implemented.

First, a statute or "pastoral provision" must be developed which will provide for some form of "common identity" (I, 2).

The Elements of Common Identity (II), at a minimum, must respect the guidelines for Structures, Liturgy, and Discipline which are specified in the letter. Cardinal Seper recognized the desire of the Bishops' Conference that the Episcopalians be absorbed into existing diocesan structures, but gave a signal that some other type of structure which is permitted by canon law and suited to the needs of the converts was not to be excluded (II, 1).

Under the heading of Discipline (II, 3), Cardinal Seper set forth several constraints concerning convert Episcopal priests: 1) They might not become bishops, 2) They might not remarry if they become widowers (some refer to this as a type of "delayed celibacy"), and 3) any future candidates for the priesthood from among the convert Episcopalians would be bound to the law of celibacy.

Episcopal priests were not immediately to be accepted as Catholic priests. Several stages had to precede acceptance. First, each candidate, according to his need, would be required to undergo theological and catechetical preparation (III, 1). The particular nature of the preparation was left to be determined. Second, each convert priest (and lay person) had to make a personal profession of faith in the teachings of the Catholic Church. This was given as an absolute condition, a *conditio sine qua non*. Third, each convert priest had to be reordained (III, 3). Reordination might not take place, however, until the CDF examined and approved each case.

Fichter[27] indicates that Cardinal Seper had given options for ordination as either absolute or conditional. On that basis Bishop Law had advised the first priest applicants in

1981 to request conditional ordination. Before action was taken on the applications by CDF, however, Cardinal Seper died and was replaced as Prefect by Cardinal Ratzinger. The applications already in Rome were returned with instructions that the applicants should seek absolute ordination. This requirement for absolute ordination, which constituted a definite rejection of the validity of Episcopal ordination, was based upon the decree *Apostolicae Curae* issued by Pope Leo XIII in 1896 in which he declared, "Anglican orders are absolutely null and utterly void."[28]

One item in the Seper letter which might easily be overlooked appears in IV which states that the pastoral provision will not be definitive (another way of saying "not permanent") but is granted *ad tempus non determinatum*. In translation this would be: for an undetermined time. That is, the pastoral provision would remain in effect as long as Rome permitted, but might be terminated at any point in the future.

The "undetermined time" has exceeded 20 years and the provision is still in effect. A point related to the issue of time is that of law. Since the pastoral provision is a time-limited exception granted to individuals, the existing canon law on celibacy did not change. All candidates for priesthood in the Western Church, other than married convert Episcopal priests, continue to be bound to perpetual celibacy.

In order to develop and subsequently to oversee implementation of the pastoral provision, the letter directs in V. 2 that an Ecclesiastical Delegate, preferably a bishop, should be designated. Although Cardinal Seper suggested strongly that Archbishop Quinn assume that position, the Bishops' Conference designated Bishop Bernard Law for the position.

In the final section of his letter, Cardinal Seper entrusts to Archbishop Quinn the manner and timing of any communication about the fact or nature of the decisions contained in the letter. In doing so, he reminds Archbishop Quinn of concerns about two sensitive areas: ecumenism and celibacy. His first concern appears directed at the possible negative impact which the pastoral provision might have on dialogue between the Catholic Church and Episcopal Church. His second concern obviously focused upon the broad question of celibacy for all priests. Since the Second Vatican Council thousands of priests had left the priesthood, a large number, though not all, because of a desire to marry. Prior to the council, the expectation had been raised among some in the Church that the rule of celibacy would be relaxed, especially in light of the strong level of acceptance for a married priesthood found in surveys of Catholics.[29] Rather than a relaxation of the canonical requirements for celibacy, the council strongly reaffirmed the Church's commitment to the discipline of a celibate priesthood.

Reportedly, the Conference of Bishops had desired to delay any announcement of approval by the Holy See until the details for implementing the pastoral provision could be worked out. However, because of an apparent information leak, the public announcement about the Seper letter was made by Archbishop Quinn at a news conference on August 20, 1980. Bishop Quinn informed the media of the contents of the Seper letter and identified Bishop Bernard Law of Springfield, MO. and Bishop Raymond Lessard of Savannah, GA. as the appointed liaisons between the Episcopal priests and the Conference of Bishops.

The next public statement about the pastoral provision was the release on March 31, 1981 of a statement by the Congregation for the Doctrine of the Faith. The statement read:

> In June 1980, the Holy See, through the Congregation for the Doctrine of the Faith, agreed to the request presented by the bishops of the United States of America on behalf of some clergy and laity formerly or actually belonging to the Episcopal (Anglican) Church for full communion with the Catholic Church. The response of the Holy See to the initiative of these Episcopalians includes the possibility of a 'pastoral provision' which will provide, for those who desire it, a common identity reflecting certain elements of their own heritage. The entrance of these persons into the Catholic Church should be understood as the 'reconciliation of those individuals who wish for full Catholic communion' of which the Decree on Ecumenism (n.4) of the Second Vatican Council speaks. In accepting former Episcopalian clergy who are married into the Catholic priesthood, the Holy See has specified that this exception to the rule of celibacy is granted in favor of these individual persons, and should not be understood as implying any change in the church's conviction of the value of priestly celibacy, which will remain the rule for future candidates for the priesthood from this group.
>
> In consultation with the National Conference of Catholic Bishops, the

Congregation for the Doctrine of the Faith has appointed the Most Rev. Bernard F. Law, bishop of Springfield-Cape Giradeau (MO.) as ecclesiastical delegate in this matter. It will be his responsibility to develop a proposal containing elements for the pastoral provision in question to be submitted for the approval of the Holy See, to oversee its implementation and to deal with the Congregation for the Doctrine of the Faith in questions pertaining to the admission of former Episcopalian clergy into the Catholic priesthood. [30]

In the months that followed, efforts to make the pastoral provision a reality in the life of the Church in the United States were ongoing, but no public information was released until Bishop Law issued a progress report on January 12, 1982, one year and a half after the Seper letter. Evidently, the direction of the Holy See that the provision be implemented "with all deliberate speed" was understood within an ecclesiastical meaning of the phrase. In Bishop Law's own words:

The Sacred Congregation for the Doctrine of the Faith, in a document dated March 31, 1981, appointed me its ecclesiastical delegate in the United States in matters pertaining to the reception of Episcopal priests and lay persons into full communion with the Roman Catholic Church. In recent months certain questions have been raised which indicate that it would be helpful for a progress report to be made.

In June of 1980, the Holy See, through the Doctrinal Congregation, agreed to a request made by the bishops of the United States on behalf of some priests and lay people formerly or actually members of the Episcopal Church for full communion. The initial requests were made by groups and individuals to local bishops and through the Apostolic Delegation in Washington. In one instance an approach was made directly to the Holy See, but was referred to the National Conference of Catholic Bishops.

The requests fall into two categories: married Episcopal priests who desire priestly ministry in the Catholic Church, and married and celibate priests who seek a common identity as former Anglicans for themselves and their parishes or lay groups.

In the public statement released in March 1981, the sacred congregation declared: "the Holy See's response to the initiative of these Episcopalians includes the possibility of a 'pastoral provision' which will provide, for those who desire it, a common identity reflecting certain elements of their own heritage.

The entrance of these persons into the Catholic Church should be understood as the 'reconciliation of those individuals who wish for full Catholic communion' of which the Decree on Ecumenism (no.4) of the Second Vatican Council speaks.

In accepting former Episcopal clergy who are married into the Catholic priesthood, the Holy See has specified that this exception to the rule of celibacy is granted in favor of these individual persons and should not be understood as implying any change in the church's conviction of the value of priestly celibacy, which will remain the rule for future candidates for the priesthood from this group.

In the fall of 1981 a three-day meeting with 26 of these petitioners was held in Dallas. This gathering included several Catholic scholars as consultors. Lectures and discussion sessions filled the days, giving a clear picture of priesthood in the Catholic Church as well as the anxieties and concerns of the Episcopalians.

During March of last year and again in November, I was in Rome to confer with officials of the Congregation for the Doctrine of the Faith. Several reports and various questions of details have been submitted in regular correspondence with that congregation.

A considerable amount of work has gone into liturgical and jurisdictional aspects of the pastoral provision, but this work has not yet reached its final form. It is presumed that jurisdictional details would receive prior concurrence of the NCCB before submission for final approval to the congregation.

It is important to point out that in every instance the church is responding to an individual's faith in the church. Even in the matter of congregations, as in the four small parishes of "the Pro-Diocese of St. Augustine of

Canterbury," the members will be received, after catechesis, as individuals.

The process being followed for the petitioners is basically in the hands of local Catholic bishops. A priest makes his application to the ordinary of a diocese, who prepares a dossier on the petitioner's personnel, academic, theological, spiritual, marital and psychological background. His statement of motive and his baptismal and ordination records are included. The dossier is sent to me, and if in proper order, transmitted to the Prefect for the Sacred Congregation for the Doctrine of the Faith as a formal petition for permission to ordain the individual candidate to the priesthood in the Catholic Church. The actual decision regarding time and place of such ordinations is the decision of the local ordinary.

It would be impossible to accurately characterize the more than 60 priests as conservative or liberal. They do not fit a mold any more easily than do Catholic priests. They are approaching the Catholic Church individually as a matter of conscience. They believe that they must be in communion with the See of Peter if they are to be fully faithful to Christ's will for the church.

While it is true that recent events in the Episcopal Church may have precipitated the decisions of some, the fact remains that a concern for Catholic faith has been operative in the lives of these petitioners for many years.

Their decision to seek full communion at this moment represents a logical development of thought. To imply that their motive is a desperate reaction to events that have occurred in the Episcopal Church or to dismiss them as "dissidents" is to fail to recognize their underlying motive of faith.

A group of scholars has assisted in preparing an assessment instrument by which to determine the special private theological study each candidate may require. A written and oral examination will certify each candidate's preparedness for ordination. To support this study program a grant has been obtained to establish an adequate lending library of theological books.

In reporting to bishops having petitioners at the Dallas meeting I wrote that "the body of Episcopalians present is representative of all those now approaching the Catholic church. Each man holds the Master's in Divinity degree from an Episcopal Church theological seminary and three have the Ph.D. degree. All but two are, or until recently were, pastors of congregations. Two are professors in colleges. There is a strong sense of joy in pastoral ministry represented among them and the Anglican tradition manifests a careful and personal concern for people.

I count it a privilege to be assisting in this work. It is gratifying that the Holy See and the bishops of the United States have responded positively to these petitioners in spite of the many questions that such positive response would inevitably raise. In no way has the response indicated a diminution of commitment to the ecumenical movement.[31]

Bishop Law began his progress report with a lengthy review of earlier information which might not be known by his reader. The new information which he provided included the fact that in the fall of 1981—over a year after the approval of the provision—he met in Dallas for three days with a group of 26 priest petitioners. No information is provided as to what contacts, if any, had been made with these individuals between July 22, 1980, the date of the Seper letter, and the time of the Dallas meeting. It is reasonable to assume that the priest petitioners were in a state of limbo during that period, having severed or greatly weakened their affiliation with the Episcopal Church and not yet having been received into the Catholic Church. In addition to the spiritual, psychological, and, in some cases, economic stress which the petitioners must have had to endure personally was added the stress upon their families.

Mary Vincent Dally, the wife of an Episcopal priest who responded immediately to the announcement of the pastoral provision, in her book[32] recounts with great feeling and attention to detail the frustrations, testing, and hardships which her husband, herself, and their children had to endure on their almost five-year journey of faith before her husband, Peter, finally was ordained as a Catholic priest. Although Cardinal Seper had admonished the Conference of Bishops that the pastoral provision was to be implemented with all deliberate speed in view of the waiting period already undergone by the Episcopalians who submitted the request, the first ordination under the provision did not take place until two years after the first announcement.

Bishop Law indirectly addressed the delay in actual implementation when he referred to having had two meetings in Rome with officials of the CDF in March and November of 1981 to confer about the provision. He noted that considerable work had been accomplished regarding liturgical and jurisdictional aspects of the pastoral provision but that final decisions had not been reached. Absent from Bishop Law's progress report was any mention of the National Conference of Catholic Bishops, although the Seper letter clearly provided that the contents of the statute or pastoral provision were to be determined with the agreement of the Episcopal Conference. One is left with the question as to what role the Bishops' Conference had in the development and subsequent approval of the contents of the pastoral provision.

The document which follows was obtained from the office of the Ecclesiastical Delegate in Boston. The document is undated and unsigned and does not appear to have been formally promulgated. It describes the process which has been and is being used to receive Episcopal clergy into the Catholic Church and to ordain them as Catholic priests.

THE PROCESS FOR EPISCOPAL PRIESTS SEEKING PRIESTHOOD IN THE CATHOLIC CHURCH[33]

1. The candidate, who is or was a priest in the Episcopal Church, directs a request for consideration of his desire for priesthood and incardination to the Bishop of the diocese of his choice.

2. The Ordinary of that diocese, should he elect to entertain the petition, interviews and investigates the candidate as he wishes.

3. The local Ordinary cooperates with the candidate in compiling a dossier which contains the required documents listed below. The candidate himself is able to provide most of the necessary documents. The Ordinary provides for the psychological or psychiatric evaluation and closes the dossier by adding to it his own letter of endorsement assuring his willingness to ordain and incardinate the petitioner with permission of the Holy See. The dossier represents a petition to the Holy See.

Contents of the Dossier

1. Covering letter from the sponsor-bishop stating his willingness to ordain the petitioner if the Congregation for the Doctrine of the Faith in Rome gives consent to the petition.

2. Petitioner's formal letter to the sponsoring Ordinary requesting priesthood in the Catholic Church.

3. Baptismal record.

4. Marriage record. If either party had been a Roman Catholic, a brief statement of the circumstances should be added to this section of the dossier.

5. Evidence of the stability and health of the marriage satisfactory to the sponsoring Ordinary.

6. A signed statement by the petitioner's wife advising of her agreement to and support of her husband's petition for priesthood in the Catholic Church.

7. Statement of the petitioner's provision for the Catholic religious education of any minor children.

8. Copy of petitioner's signed Profession of Faith if he has been received into full communion with the See of Peter at the time the dossier is submitted.

9. Seminary and other graduate school transcripts.

10. Evidence of ordination in the Episcopal Church and succession list of ordaining prelate.

11. Psychiatric evaluation report (the MMPI is recommended as a minimum psychological test).

12. Biographical sketch written by petitioner. (This should include religion of parents, number of siblings, childhood religious environment, motives for seeking full communion with Catholic Church, motives for desiring Catholic Priestly Ministry, background of marriage, and other important factors in present decision as well as brief biographical data.)

13. If there are any pertinent documents or letters of reference, they would constitute an item number 13.

All documents may be photo copies. A dossier should have each document clearly identified. There should be a typed Table of Contents having each item numbered and described in a manner similar to the list above. A plain sheet having the description typed in the center and the corresponding number near the top right corner should be placed in the dossier before each document. All handwritten items should be followed by typed copy of the text. The dossier should be enclosed in a Duo-Tang three hole binder.

4. Three sets of the dossier should be sent to the Cardinal Ecclesiastical Delegate of the Congregation for the Doctrine of the Faith by the sponsoring ordinary. (When a petitioner provides documents for a dossier, he should be

aware of how many copies his sponsoring Ordinary may require for diocesan files.) Submission address is:

> His Eminence Bernard Cardinal Law
> Archbishop of Boston &
> Ecclesiastical Delegate
> 2101 Commonwealth Avenue
> Brighton, Massachusetts 02135

5.The Ecclesiastical Delegate reviews the dossier to see if all documents are in order. If no adjustments or additions are required, the Delegate writes a letter of submission noting any pertinent facts known to himself.

6. With the Ecclesiastical Delegate's submission letter attached, two copies of the dossier are transmitted to the Congregation for the Doctrine of the Faith by the Pronuncio's diplomatic pouch.

7. One copy of the dossier remains in the files of the Ecclesiastical Delegate.

8. Should the sponsoring Ordinary have correspondence for the Doctrinal Congregation regarding his dossier petition after submission, it should be sent to the office of the Ecclesiastical Delegate who would forward it with a letter from the Delegate.

9. Priestly Formation - Theological:

When a local Ordinary submits a dossier, he directs the candidate's participation in the assessment-study-certification process of theological formation. The process is as follows:

Guidelines for Local Ordinaries

A. The Assessment Instrument is a syllabus of theological topics of which each petitioner is expected to have sufficient knowledge. He receives a copy of the Instrument and meets with an assessment team of theologians. The interview is oral and involves specific questions by the assessors who provide a written report to the petitioner and his sponsoring Ordinary, pointing out areas in which further study is indicated. The Ecclesiastical Delegate arranges for the Assessment conference and advises the sponsoring Ordinary. This is not an examination.

B. The Bibliography is a list of theological books compiled by the Ecclesiastical Delegate's theological consultors and is designed to include all topics on The Assessment Instrument. In the assessment interview the assessors can review with the petitioner the bibliography and highlight those titles which may involve reading sections of various books or the books in their entirety which pertain to the needs. It is not presumed that anyone will study the entire bibliography. The entire list of books forms St. Bede's Theological Library at 1841 Wilshire Drive, Charleston, SC 29407. These books may be borrowed by mail. The local Ordinary should appoint a learned priest to guide the petitioner's study. It is understood that the time required for study depends upon the petitioner's need and available time.

10. When the Congregation for the Doctrine of the Faith issues a <u>Rescript</u> permitting ordination, the Ecclesiastical Delegate communicates this fact to the petitioner's sponsoring Ordinary.

A. <u>The Certification Examination</u> is the conclusion of the process and is intended to assure the local Ordinary that the petitioner is theologically qualified for ordination as a Catholic priest. This exam may be taken as soon as a <u>Rescript</u> (consent to the dossier) is received from the Congregation for the Doctrine of the Faith and the petitioner is prepared. The petitioner should understand that he is responsible for the entire syllabus.

B. The Certification Examination consists of two parts. A written exam will be sent to the Ordinary who oversees its administration in the petitioner's place of residence. After the completed exam is read by the theological team, a date is arranged for the oral portion of this final exam and the petitioner again meets with the team. The office of the Ecclesiastical Delegate makes all arrangements for the Certification Examination.

11. It is presumed that the local Ordinary would pay expenses incurred by the Assessment and the Certification Examination (i.e., travel, lodging, photo copying, etc.). The

Ecclesiastical Delegate's office will advise the Ordinary of costs after such meetings.

12. Priestly Formation - Spiritual:

The local Ordinary should appoint a capable priest to meet regularly with the petitioner. The priest would serve as a formation director and a source of support for the petitioner.

13. If the petitioner is not already in full communion with the Catholic Church, at some time during the process it is expected that plans would be made to do this. This should be done as soon as possible and practicable. Confirmation is part of this reception.

14. The Holy See expects that a petitioner should experience full communion for a year before he would be ordained. The sponsoring Ordinary may petition the Congregation for the Doctrine of the Faith (through the office of the Ecclesiastical Delegate) for a reduction of this time after a Rescript is issued and the Certification Examination is completed if he has sufficient pastoral reason.

15. When a Rescript is received from the Congregation for the Doctrine of the Faith, and when the petitioner has satisfactorily completed the Certification Examination and any other requirements imposed by the local Ordinary are met, the petitioner may be ordained Deacon then Priest by his Ordinary. He is incardinated in the usual manner.

16. The petitioner is expected to maintain close contact with the Assistant to the Ecclesiastical Delegate.

17. In every step the Ecclesiastical Delegate's office is prepared to offer assistance and guidance to the local Ordinary and to the petitioner.

The exact date when and the manner in which the pastoral provision became an operational reality are uncertain. What is known is that the first priest ordained under authority of the provision on June 29, 1982, was Father James Parker, one of the earliest Episcopalian petitioners who contacted Archbishop Jardot in 1977. Father Parker, a married father of two children, was ordained quietly by Bishop Law for the Diocese of Charleston, South Carolina.

After ordination, rather than being assigned to the Charleston diocese, Father Parker assumed a position as assistant to Bishop Law for the pastoral provision. Father Parker's wife, Alma, took on responsibility for managing the lending library of theological books which the above cited process refers to as St. Bede's library.

When Bishop Law became Archbishop of Boston in 1984 (and subsequently Cardinal in 1985), Father Parker moved with him and continued in his capacity as assistant to the Ecclesiastical Delegate until 1995. Presently, Father Parker serves as pastor of the Church of the Holy Spirit in South Carolina. In his capacity as pastor, Father Parker is one of only two pastors[34] among the married priests who converted from the Episcopal Church, other than those priests who are pastors of the several "Anglican-use Parishes" which will be discussed in the next section.

When the Holy See approved the pastoral provision, the Congregation for the Doctrine of the Faith stated clearly that priest converts from the Episcopal Church were not to be named as canonical pastors. Preferably, they were to be given assignments to other priestly duties: hospital chaplaincy, campus ministry, prison ministry, teaching, or in some instances, parish assistants. According to one pastoral provision priest, the Holy See was asked more than once why convert married priests were prohibited from being named pastors. However, an answer was not provided.

> As of July 31, 1989, Hill reported:
> 37 married Episcopalians have been ordained absolutely.
> 12 unmarried Episcopalian priests have gone through the PP and have been ordained.
> An unknown number of other unmarried Episcopalian priests have been ordained without going through PP.
> No married priests have left the ordained ministry.
> *Note:*CDF recommends to bishops that unmarried Episcopalian priests also prepare themselves by means of the PP process. Their dossiers, of course, are not sent to CDF because these men are unmarried and are not otherwise impaired.
>
> How many candidates were there for ordination? Hill reported that:
> 12 dossiers were in the hands of CDF awaiting issuance of the rescript.
> 18 dossiers were in the process of being assembled.[35]

Hill could not report an absolute number of unmarried Episcopal priests who had converted and been ordained as

Catholic priests because no central clearinghouse existed then, or now, to capture this type of information. As he noted, unmarried convert Episcopal priests were under no canonical restraints which would require approval from the Holy See. Once they entered the Catholic Church they did not differ from any other celibate male Catholic for purposes of ordination.

Reverend William H. Stetson, Secretary to Cardinal Law for the Pastoral Provision, in a letter to the author on April 6, 2000 provided the following updated information:[36]

> Seventy-three men have been ordained under the Pastoral Provision. This figure includes twelve celibate men who, by way of exception, were allowed to use the Pastoral Provision process. Of the seventy-three, five were assigned as pastor to a personal parish established under the Pastoral Provision, and one is chaplain to a parish in formation. Two married men have been granted permission by the Holy See to be appointed pastor of a territorial parish. One of these is Father James Parker. Finally, one man has recently passed the certification examination and is preparing for ordination and one dossier is presently in Rome. Two dossiers are in preparation.

UNITS OF COMMON IDENTITY

The leaders of four small Episcopal congregations that separated from the Episcopal Church following the Minneapolis General Convention and formed the Pro-Diocese of St. Augustine of Canterbury had a vision. They proposed to bring all members of their respective congregations, and other separated Episcopalians, into the Catholic Church through a form of corporate act. In effect, when the leaders of the Pro-Diocese met in Rome with Cardinal Seper, they presented the concept of a Uniate Anglican Church comprised of former Episcopalians who would come into full reconciliation with the Roman Catholic Church while being permitted to retain a degree of self-governance and continued cultural identity similar, they believed, to the situation of the Eastern Churches that were in union with Rome.

Although the Holy See did not accept the concept of a new Uniate Church, Cardinal Seper did extend the possibility that Episcopalians might be permitted to preserve some form of common identity. In his letter to Archbishop Quinn, Cardinal Seper directed that:

> 2) It will be appropriate to formulate a statute or "pastoral provision" which provides for a "common identity" for the group.

While Cardinal Seper did not detail the nature of the common identity, he did set ground rules for the American Bishops to follow in the areas of structures and liturgy.

II. Elements of the "Common Identity"

1) <u>Structures</u>: the preference expressed by the majority of the Episcopal Conference for the insertion of these reconciled Episcopalians into the diocesan structures under the jurisdiction of the local Ordinaries is recognized. Nevertheless, the possibility of some other type of structure as provided for by canonical dispositions, and as suited to the needs of the group, is not excluded.

2) <u>Liturgy</u>: The group may retain certain elements of the Anglican liturgy; these are to be determined by a Commission of the Congregation set up for this purpose. Use of these elements will be reserved to the former members of the Anglican Communion. Should a former Anglican priest celebrate public liturgy outside this group, he will be required to adopt the common Roman Rite.

<u>COMMON IDENTITY CONGREGATIONS</u>

Our Lady of the Atonement in the Archdiocese of San Antonio[37] was the first parish erected under the "common identity" authority of the pastoral provision. On August 15, 1983, the Most Reverend Patrick F. Flores, Archbishop of San Antonio, received a small group of eighteen converts from the Episcopal Church into the Catholic Church. These few people were the founding members of Our Lady of the Atonement Parish. The Reverend Christopher G. Phillips, a married former Episcopal priest with two children, was among the converts. As a part of the overall ceremony of reception, Archbishop Flores ordained Father Phillips as a Catholic Priest and named him to be the pastor of this first parish established under the pastoral provision with permission to follow elements of the Anglican liturgical heritage while being fully recognized as a Catholic parish.

Our Lady of the Atonement, and other congregations which followed, are referred to variously as "Anglican-use Parishes," "Personal Parishes," or "Common Identity" parishes. The pastoral provision granted to individual Ordinaries the authority to establish such congregations based upon the authority of Canon 518 of the Code of Canon Law which states:

> **Personal Parishes**
> Canon 518: As a general rule, a parish is to be territorial, that is, it is to embrace all Christ's faithful of a given territory. Where it is useful, however, personal parishes are to be established, determined by reason of the rite, language or nationality of the faithful of a certain territory, or on some other basis.

In the years since the parish was erected, Father Phillips continues as the pastor and in February 2000 reported on the vibrant nature of the parish. The number of parishioners had grown from 18 to slightly in excess of 1,200; a parish school attracted young families to the parish which gave the assurance of another generation of young people growing up within the context of the pastoral provision; and there were tentative plans to establish a high school. Father Phillips noted that growth in the number of parishioners had made it necessary to consider expanding the size of the church building.[38]

Clearly, over time the element of the pastoral provision which originally limited membership of the

Anglican-use parishes to converts from the Episcopal Church has given way to a more open approach as to who may attend.

Our Lady of Walsingham in Houston, Texas, was the second parish recognized as an Anglican- use congregation.[39] The parish owes its name to the English national shrine of Walsingham which traces its origins back to 1061.

In the fall of 1981, Father James Moore, a married Episcopal priest, attended a three-day meeting of 26 applicants for the Catholic priesthood whom Bishop Law gathered at Holy Trinity Seminary in Dallas. With the assistance of Catholic scholars, the meeting participants sought to obtain a clear picture of priesthood in the Catholic Church and to address the concerns and anxieties of the participants about transition from the Episcopal Church. During the meeting the petitioners were informed of the studies which would be required, based upon the background of each petitioner; and the procedures were clarified for their reception into the Catholic Church and subsequent ordination to Catholic priesthood.

Father Moore was released from his Episcopal responsibilities by his bishop and moved with his wife to Houston. In 1982 they gathered a group of interested persons and took the first informal steps toward their hoped for establishment of an Anglican-use parish. Finally, in 1984 Father Moore, his wife, and the others of their informal congregation were received into the Catholic Church. A month later Bishop Fiorenza ordained Father Moore as a Catholic priest and named him as pastor of Our Lady of Walsingham which was formally erected as the second Anglican-use parish on April 7, 1984. Father Moore continues to serve as pastor as of this writing.

Father Clark Tea,[40] a celibate Episcopal priest, who had been among those who met with Cardinal Seper in 1979, sought to establish an Anglican-use parish in Las Vegas, Nevada. After a prolonged period of waiting, Father Tea and about 25 of his former parishioners were received into the Catholic Church in September 1983. Two additional years passed before the Anglican-use parish of Saint Mary the Virgin was dedicated on May 26, 1985. The small parish struggled for a number of years but suffered from attrition until on July 1, 1997 the diocese reduced the parish to a mission status before finally terminating the mission on March 6, 1998.

Two more recent examples of Anglican-use congregations are St. Mary the Virgin parish in Arlington, Texas,[41] and the Congregation of St. Athanasius in West Roxbury, Massachusetts.[42]

The history of St. Mary the Virgin dates back to 1961 when it was established as a mission within the Episcopal Church. In 1969 it was elevated to parish status. In 1980 The Reverend Allan R.G. Hawkins, a married priest with two children, was named rector of the parish. Six years later the parish was named St. Mary the Virgin. A new church building was built in 1990.

In the summer of 1991 the parish decided to withdraw from the Episcopal Church and to seek full communion with the Roman Catholic Church under the pastoral provision. On June 12, 1994, Bishop Joseph P. Delaney, Bishop of Fort Worth, received about 120 members of the parish into the Catholic Church. In reality, the actual number of persons in the congregation exceeded 120 since some parishioners who had been born Catholics but, for one reason or another, had become Episcopalians, made a return journey to the religion of their birth. A few days later, Bishop Delaney ordained Father Hawkins to the Catholic priesthood.

A unique aspect of the story of St. Mary the Virgin is that not only did the parishioners personally enter the Catholic Church, they transferred corporately into the Catholic Church, and in the process brought with them the parish property, including the church building which Bishop Delaney dedicated as a Catholic parish in October, 1994.

Within a few years the parishioners at St. Mary the Virgin had more than tripled to over 600, with average Sunday mass attendance of between 350 and 400. Father Hawkins believes that some of the growth has come from Catholics who have joined because they like the liturgical and spiritual "style" of the parish. He adds that the parish has proved to be an "accessible doorway" into the Church not only for Anglicans but also for those who come from other Reformation traditions.

The most recently established congregation for Anglican-use is the Congregation of St. Athanasius in the Archdiocese of Boston. This congregation began when several dozen members of the Episcopal Parish of All Saints in the Dorchester section of Boston, together with their rector, The Reverend Richard Sterling Bradford, decided in January 1996 to withdraw from the Episcopal Church and seek corporate admission into the Roman Catholic Church. After a period of preparation, 29 persons were received into the Catholic Church on September 28, 1997. The Reverend Bradford, who is married, subsequently was ordained as a Catholic priest and serves as chaplain to the congregation.

At the present time the congregation does not have a church of its own and conducts services at Saint Theresa Convent Chapel in West Roxbury, Massachusettes.

In addition to the congregations which have been described, the web site of the Pastoral Provision Office lists the following Anglican-use congregations: St. Thomas More Parish, Fort Worth, Texas; Church of the Good Shepherd Parish, Columbia, South Carolina; St. Margaret of Scotland Parish, Austin, Texas; and St. Anselm Community, Corpus Christi, Texas.[43] The former pastor of one listed congregation indicated that the congregation is no longer functional.

Some Anglican-use parishes have grown over the years; others, such as St. Mary the Virgin in Las Vegas, have struggled and not survived. For congregations that have grown, expansion has come primarily from the children of the first converts or from Catholics in the general population who have been attracted to the "liturgy and style" of the Anglican-use congregations. However, even the successful parishes face an uncertain future.

The letter of April 7, 2000 from the Pastoral Provision office indicated that a total of 73 priests have been ordained under the pastoral provision. The table on the next pages provides the names, dioceses, and ordination dates of the priests.

Pastoral Provision Priests		
Name	**Diocese**	**Year**
Rev. Bradley Barber	Corpus Christi	1994
Rev. Bruce Bowes	New York	1992
Rev. Richard Bradford	Boston	1998
Rev. Winthrop Brainard	Washington, D.C.	1987
Rev. Timothy Alan Church	Dallas	1995
Rev. Richard G. Cipolla	Bridgeport	1984
Rev. John L. Congdon	Fresno	2000
Rev. John L. Cowart	Dallas	1984
Rev. John D. Culpepper	Tyler	1983
Rev. Peter F. Dally	Tulsa	1985
Rev. David M. Dye	Atlanta	1992
Rev. Patrick Eastman	Tulsa	1984
Rev. John Ellis	Venice	1991
Rev. James Lee Evans	Austin	1994
Rev. Larch W. Fidler IV	St. Louis/Portland	1987
Rev. Joseph H. Frazer	Austin	1987
Rev. Robert R. Freed	Wichita	1984
Rev. James Furlong	Lubuck	1984
Rev. C. Lee Gilbertson	Springfield, MA	1986
Rev. Charles W. Graves	Baker	1985
Rev. Paul F. Gray	Dallas	1985
Rev. George G. Greenway	Springfield, MA	1987
Rev. John G. Gremmeis	Fort Worth	1991
Rev. Lee W. Gross	Arlington	1987
Rev. Chester Hand	Austin	1986
Rev. Addison H. Hart	Rockford	1999
Rev. E. James Hart	Fort Worth	1996
Rev. Allan R.G. Hawkins	Fort Worth	1994
Rev. Scott Hurd	Washington, D.C.	1999
Rev. Dennis Kuhn	Charlotte	1984
Rev. William D.Ladkau	Charleston	1984

Rev. William T. Lawson	San Diego	1986
Rev. William Lipscomb	Gaylord, MI	1997
Rev. Paul E. Lockey	Boston	1987
Rev. Douglas Lorig	Phoenix	1984
Rev. Larry D. Losing	Orlando	1984
Rev. George C. Mc Cormick	Camden	1987
Rev. Robert Mc Elwee	Wichita	1983
Rev. James Mc Ghee	Amarillo	1995
Rev. Walter Mitchell	Miami	1991
Rev. James T. Moore	Houston	1984
Rev. Lloyd Dean Morris	Dallas	1995
Rev. William Muniz	Miami	1994
Rev. Daniel Munn	Savannah	1982
Rev. John Neff	Erie	1986
Rev. Trevor Nicholls	New York	1990
Rev. Robert Ninedorf	Charleston	1989
Rev. Marc K. Oliver	New York	1989
Rev. James Parker	Charleston	1982
Rev. Robert A. Pearson	Trenton	1986
Rev. Christopher G. Phillips	San Antonio	1983
Rev. Randall Scott Rainwater	Stockton	1996
Rev. James Ramsey	Houston	1984
Rev. Peter Reynierse	Washington, D.C.	1994
Rev. Alan E. Rosenau	Little Rock	1988
Rev. Thad B. Rudd	Atlanta	1991
Rev. Raymond O. Ryland	San Diego	1983
Rev. James W. Samter	Green Bay	1987
Rev. Robert Santry	Honolulu	1986
Rev. Robert T. Schriber	Raleigh	1996
Rev. James Sharp	Dallas	1984
Rev. Gary Sherman	Tulsa	1985
Rev. W. Bry Shields	Mobile	1984
Rev. David E. Staal	Oakland	1990
Rev. David Stokes	Providence	****

Rev. Stephen R. Sutton	Baltimore	1984
Rev. Gordon Taylor	Boise	1985
Rev. Paul van K. Thomson	Providence	1983
Rev. Grover Tipton	St. Augustine	1996
Rev. Richard Turner	Raleigh	1991
Rev. Peter F. Watterson	Palm Beach	1987
Rev. Leo G. Weishaar	Mobile	1984
Rev. John L. Whitsell	Kilgore, TX	1996
Rev. William L. Winston	Paterson	1986
**** In process		

A total of 48 dioceses are represented in the table. Two priests were ordained in 1982, the first year of pastoral provision ordinations. The largest number ordained in a single year was 15 in 1984. More than half of all ordinations took place between 1982 - 1987.

Except for those priests assigned to minister to the Anglican-use congregations, only two pastoral provision priests have been assigned with the permission of the Holy See to be pastors of parishes serving the general Catholic population.[44]

> Hill explains:
> It is also the policy of the CDF that these married priests may not be assigned to what is called, 'the ordinary care of souls (*cura ordinaria animarium*).' This implies that they are not to be assigned to full-time parochial ministry, but should be employed as chaplains, teachers, administrators and the like. At the same time, however, they also exercise the ordained ministry in parishes - celebrating the Eucharist, preaching, hearing confessions, etc.[45]

One pastoral provision priest indicated that the Holy See had been asked on at least two occasions for the reason why these priests were restricted from assignments to the ordinary care of souls. Reportedly, the Holy See chose not to respond to the question. Perhaps some indication of the reason may be found in Cardinal Seper's letter to Archbishop Wright.

> Cardinal Seper wrote:
> 3) Discipline: (a) To married Episcopalian priests who may be ordained Catholic priests, the following stipulations will apply: they may not become bishops; and they may not remarry in case of widowhood. (b) Future candidates for the priesthood must follow the discipline of celibacy. (c) Special care must be taken on the

pastoral level to avoid any misunderstanding regarding the Church's discipline of celibacy.

In closing Cardinal Seper added:
I am sure you will have already noted in the decisions as reported a concern for the sensitive areas of ecumenism and celibacy.

The staunch defense of celibacy appears not only in the direct references but in the restriction on remarriage for widowed priests found in the Seper letter. This provision has been referred to as a form of "delayed celibacy."

In the absence of an official explanation of the restriction, one is led to believe that perhaps the Holy See was anxious lest the general Catholic population which was not accustomed to a married priesthood might be scandalized or offended to have the wife and children of a priest sitting in a church pew while a priest husband and father (parent) celebrated mass. Or one might conjecture that the Vatican was concerned that the presence of even a few married pastors among the predominantly celibate pastors might undermine the Church's position that only a celibate priesthood can perfectly model the presence of Christ the High Priest and Good Shepherd (Pastor).

Repeated surveys over several decades have documented that, rather than being scandalized, a large majority of Catholics favor the option of married priests.[46] As witness to the possibility of married pastors modeling the ideal priesthood of Christ, one need only look to Peter and countless others in the early Church, or to the two-thousand-year tradition of married pastors in the Eastern Churches.

The permission for the pastoral provision was given for an undetermined period of time. That period has exceeded twenty years and there have been no public signs that the Holy See is about to rescind the provision. However, as shown by the data in the above table and confirmed by the letter of April 7, 2000 from the Pastoral Provision Office, the numbers of new applicants for Catholic priesthood under the pastoral provision has reduced to a trickle. Therefore, a critical question for the future of Anglican-use congregations is: Where will the next generation of priests versed in the unique culture and liturgy of their tradition come from?

The pastoral provision explicitly requires that any vocations to the priesthood from the Anglican-use parishes must be trained in the Latin Rite and be subject to the rule of celibacy. No plan exists to assure the continuance of ministry to Anglican-use congregations when the priests who presently serve them retire, become disabled, or die.

Apparently, in granting the pastoral provision, the Holy See envisioned either: 1) that the Anglican-use congregations would phase out as the original parishioners died or were integrated into the mainstream parishes; or 2) that a continuous flow of priest converts coming from the Episcopal Church would be willing to serve the Anglican-use communities.

If the pastoral provision was given under the first assumption, the reality of twenty years experience has shown the assumption to have been erroneous. For reasons mentioned above, some Anglican-use parishes not only have not diminished, but have prospered in their overall membership. If the pastoral provision was granted under the second assumption, the data cited in the above table and letter from the Pastoral Provision Office do not support the assumption. Most priest converts have chosen to be integrated into the majority Catholic population, rather than serve Anglican-use congregations. According to the April 7,

2000 letter from the Pastoral Provision Office ". . . one man has recently passed the certification examination and is preparing for ordination and one dossier is presently in Rome. Two dossiers are in preparation." There is no assurance that any of the four priest candidates will choose to minister to an Anglican-use congregation.

CANADA

In October of 1986 the Canadian Conference of Catholic Bishops by unanimous request petitioned the Holy See for the approval of pastoral provision norms identical to those already approved for the United States. Cardinal Joseph Ratzinger, Prefect of the Congregation for the Doctrine of the Faith, informed Bishop Bernard Hubert by letter on December 15, 1986, that the request of the Canadian Bishops had been approved.[47] (A copy of the complete text of the letter and other documents cited in this section follow beginning at page 110).

Cardinal Ratzinger in the last paragraph of the letter reminded Bishop Hubert of a point discussed at their last meeting: "namely, that a comprehensive study of the whole situation regarding the ordination to the priesthood of married former Anglican and other clergy requires to be undertaken by this congregation." The reminder is of interest because Pope Paul VI in his encyclical *Sacerdotalis caelibatus* n. 42 written in 1967 first indicated the appropriateness of such a study.[48] Clearly the study had not been undertaken at the time of the Ratzinger letter, or, apparently, at any later date.

After a few years of experience using the identical process as the United States, the Canadian Conference of Catholic Bishops in June 1991 prepared and submitted to the Holy See a Canadian version of the process. The Canadian version included minor revisions in the order of the content and made appropriate semantic changes. In only one area did the Canadian version differ substantively from the United States version. Cardinal Ratzinger sent a letter of approval for the revised Canadian procedures to Bishop Marcel Gervais,

President of the Canadian Conference of Catholic Bishops, on April 13, 1992.[49] The title of the Canadian procedures is:

The Process for Married Anglican Priests Seeking Priesthood in the Catholic Church.[50]

Some of the differences between the United States and Canadian versions are noted below. Side-by-side comparison can be made by referring to the United States version at pages 81-88 and the complete Canadian version at pages 113-118.

1. The first difference between the two versions is the designation of applicants.

The process in the United States refers to petitioners as "Episcopal priests." The Canadian process refers to petitioners as "married Anglican priests." While the Episcopal Church in the United States has its roots in Anglicanism, it is organizationally independent from the Anglican Church. The history and nature of this distinction are beyond the scope of this discussion. One point, however, is relevant.

The wording of the process in the United States easily leads to a conclusion that the pastoral provision covers all Episcopal priests who petition for ordination as Catholic priests. In actuality, the pastoral provision refers solely to married Episcopal priests. Unmarried Episcopal priests who enter into full communion with the Catholic Church and seek Catholic ordination are no different for purposes of ordination from other unmarried Catholic layman. Nonetheless, as Hill notes: CDF recommends to bishops that unmarried Episcopalian priests also prepare themselves by means of the PP process. Their dossiers, of course, are not sent to CDF because these men are unmarried and are not otherwise impeded.[51]

The data received from the Episcopal Delegate in the United States indicate that 12 unmarried Episcopal priests have followed the recommendation of the CDF and have gone through the pastoral provision process. 'It is not known how many, if any, others were ordained without going through the process since no clearinghouse exists to collect such data.

The Canadian process avoids ambiguity in the matter by clearly identifying subjects of the pastoral provision as married Anglican priests. Information is not available as to whether CDF made any recommendation to the Canadian Conference of Catholic Bishops regarding the use of the pastoral provision by unmarried Anglican priests seeking Catholic ordination.

A second difference appears in the requirements concerning prior ordination.

The process for the United States (n.10) requires the petitioner to submit evidence of ordination in the Episcopal Church and the succession list of the ordaining prelate. The Canadian process requires evidence of ordination in the Anglican Church (N. 11) but does not require submission of the succession list of the ordaining prelate. The Canadian process is consistent with the requirement of the Holy See that all petitioners must be ordained absolutely. The required submission of the succession list of the ordaining Episcopal prelate by each United States candidate is irrelevant since all ordinations are give absolutely, not conditionally.

The requirement for absolute ordination is based on the 1896 papal bull *Apostolicae Curae* where Pope Leo XIII declared Anglican orders "absolutely null and utterly void."

The third and only substantive difference between the two processes concerns the issue of financial support.

The United States process is silent as to any arrangements concerning the financial support of married priests and their families. The matter is left to each individual bishop to determine. Meanwhile, the Canadian process provides clear and strong assurances, as follows:

> 11. The sponsoring bishop shall make suitable provisions for registration of the newly-ordained cleric in the diocesan pension plan, and shall determine that suitable arrangements have been made for the support of the cleric's wife and family in the event of the priest's subsequent death or disability.

In addition to the guidelines governing the process for married Anglican priests who seek priesthood in the Roman Catholic Church, the Canadian Conference of Catholic Bishops has developed and promulgated in cooperation with the Canadian Anglican Church a unique document entitled:

PASTORAL GUIDELINES FOR CHURCHES IN THE CASE OF CLERGY MOVING FROM ONE COMMUNION TO ANOTHER.[52]

The first paragraph of this document reads:

> 1. In Canada over the past few years there have been instances of Anglican or Roman Catholic clergy joining the other church and wishing to exercise an ordained ministry. Sometimes there have been unfortunate consequences, resulting in uncertainty and confusion among

members of both churches. The individuals concerned are motivated by deep personal reasons but people do not always understand what has happened or why. We hope that such transitions might not be occasions of triumphalism but will take place in ways appropriate to a relationship between two churches which today receive each other as sister churches in real but imperfect communion. For this reason, it will be helpful to both churches in such cases to deal with each other openly and in a spirit of collaboration and by so doing give a sign of mutual respect to the world.

The *Pastoral Guidelines* develop the theme identified in the first paragraph under four major headings: I. Ordained Ministry in the Life of the Church, II. Communication between Bishops, III. Following Appropriate Procedures, IV. Pastoral Support for Those in Transition. The *Guidelines* clearly and respectfully recognize that the movement of Catholic and Anglican clergy is in both directions and that in this matter, as in all else, the Church is called to proclaim the reconciling love of God in Christ.

The text of each document is given on the following pages. The documents are: Cardinal Ratzinger First Approval Letter, December 15, 1986; Cardinal Ratzinger Second Approval Letter, April 13, 1992; the Process for Married Anglican Priests Seeking Priesthood in the Roman Catholic Church; and the Pastoral Guidelines for Chuches in the Case of Clergy Moving from One Communion to Another.

15 December 1986

CONGREGATIO
PRO DOCTRINA FIDEI

Prot. N. 159/84 Disc.

Your Excellency,

With your letter of 12 October, for which many   thanks, you
put to this Congregation the unanimous request of the Canadian
Conference of Catholic Bishops for the approval for Canada of the norms
already conceded to the Bishops' Conference of the United States
regarding the admission of married former Anglican clergymen for
ordination to priesthood.

As far as the aforesaid norms apply to a bishop's sponsoring
of an individual candidate as described, and under the same
conditions listed on the Holy See's rescript for ordination
(with which you are familiar), the Congregation is pleased to
confirm its favourable response to your request.

This particular approval notwithstanding, Your Excellency will no doubt
call to mind a point raised by us in our meeting of 30 October last:
namely, that a comprehensive study of the whole situation regarding the
ordination to priesthood of married former Anglican and other clergy
requires to be undertaken by this Congregation.

With kindest regards and cordial sentiments of esteem,
I remain,

Sincerely yours in Christ,

Joseph Cardinal Ratzinger

His Excellency
The Right Rev. Bernard HUBERT

CONGREGATIO
PRO DOCTRINA FIDEI

00193 Romae,   **April 13, 1992**
Piazza del S. Uffizio, 11

159/84 Disc.

Prot. N.
(In responsione fiat mentio huius numeri)

Your Excellency:

Please excuse the delay in responding to the letter sent by your Episcopal Conference to this Congregation on November 4th of last year with reference to the revised process proposed for considering petitions coming from former Anglican clergymen in Canada who are married and seek ordination as Catholic priests. The norms for such cases, adapted to the Canadian situation, had already been approved in the main by this Dicastery's letter sent to your predecessor, Bishop Robert Lebel, on December 14, 1990 under the same protocol number above.

This Congregation is pleased that the Canadian Bishops have chosen to incorporate into the process the figure of an ecclesiastical delegate who would assure a uniform and precise fulfillment of the norms and act as an intermediary between this Dicastery and the sponsoring Ordinaries for the sake of expediting communications and clarifications as needed. We are also quite happy to accept the Permanent Council's suggestion of Bishop Anthony Tonnos, the Ordinary of Hamilton, as one who could well fulfill that role. We will look forward to working with Bishop Tonnos as our Ecclesiastical Delegate in Canada for such cases.

Your Excellency may recall that this Dicastery was interested in receiving a copy of the "Assessment Instrument" which would be used to evaluate the theological readiness of candidates of this kind along with the "reading list" and "certification examination" prepared for them. It would also appreciate learning who will be designated as the Bishops' theological consultants for the fashioning of these various diagnostic tools.

Most Reverend Marcel Gervais
President
Canadian Conference of Catholic Bishops
CANADA

111

CALL AND RESPONSE

Realizing, of course, that the ultimate form of such instruments awaits the direction and approval of the Ecclesiastical Delegate, we would hope that Bishop Tonnos will soon be in a position to advise us in this regard.

Assuring your Excellency of kindest regards and with prayerful best wishes for the Feast of Easter, I am

Sincerely yours in Christ,

Joseph Cardinal Ratzinger

Received
May 5. 1992

Canadian Conference of Catholic Bishops

The Process for Married Anglican Priests Seeking Priesthood In The Roman Catholic Church

1. The married candidate, who is or was a priest in the Anglican Church, directs a request for consideration of his desire for priesthood and incardination to the bishop of the diocese of his choice.

2   The diocesan bishop of that diocese, should he elect to entertain the petition, interviews and investigates the candidate as he wishes.

3. This sponsoring bishop cooperates with the candidate in compiling a dossier which contains the required documents listed below. The candidate himself is able to provide most of the necessary documents. The sponsoring bishop provides for the psychological evaluation and closes the dossier by adding to it his own letter of endorsement assuring his willingness to ordain and incardinate the petitioner with permission of the Holy See. The dossier represents a petition to the Holy See.

Contents of dossier

1. The petitioner's formal letter to the sponsoring bishop requesting priesthood in the Catholic Church.

2. Covering letter from the sponsoring bishop stating his willingness to ordain the petitioner if the Congregation for the Doctrine of the Faith gives consent to the petition, and his views as to the candidate's future ministry.

3. Biographical sketch written by the petitioner. (This should include religion of parents, childhood religious environment, motives for seeking full communion with the Catholic Church, motives for desiring Catholic priestly ministry, background of marriage, and other important factors in his present decision as well as brief biographical data).

4. Baptismal record

5. Marriage record. If either party had been a Roman Catholic, a brief statement of the circumstances should be added to this section of the dossier.

6. Evidence of the stability and health of the marriage satisfactory to the sponsoring bishop.

7. A signed statement by the petitioner's wife advising of her agreement to and support of her husband's petition for priesthood in the Catholic Church.

8. Statement of the petitioner's provision for the Catholic religious education of any minor children.

9. Copy of petitioner's signed Profession of Faith if he has been received into full communion

> with the See of Peter at the time the dossier is
> submitted.
> 10. Seminary and other graduate school transcripts.
> 11. Evidence of ordination in the Anglican Church.
> 12. Psychological evaluation report (the MMPI is
> recommended as a minimum psychological
> test).
> 13. If there are any pertinent documents or letters
> of reference, they would constitute item
> number 13.

4. All documents may be photocopies. The dossier
should have each document clearly identified. There
should be a typed Table of Contents having each item
numbered and described in a manner similar to the list
above. A plain sheet having the description typed in
the center and the corresponding number near the top
right corner should be placed in the dossier before
each document. All handwritten items should be
followed by a typed copy of the text.

5. Three sets of dossiers should be sent to the
Ecclesiastical Delegate of the Congregation for the
Doctrine of the Faith by the sponsoring bishop. The
Ecclesiastical Delegate will review the dossier carefully.
If all documents are in order, he will write a letter of
presentation, noting also any pertinent facts known to
himself.

6. With the Ecclesiastical Delegate's letter of presentation
attached, two (2) copies of the dossier are sent to the
Congregation for the Doctrine of the Faith. One (1)
copy of the dossier is kept in the files of the
Ecclesiastical Delegate.

7.   Priestly Formation — Theological.
After the dossier is submitted to the Congregation, the sponsoring bishop directs the candidate's participation in the assessment-study-certification process of theological formation. The process is as follows:

A.   The Assessment Instrument is a syllabus of theological topics of which each petitioner is expected to have a sufficient knowledge. He receives a copy of the Instrument and meets with an assessment team of theologians (usually professors in a Faculty of Theology). This interview is oral and involves specific questions by the assessors who provide a written report to the petitioner and his sponsoring bishop, pointing out areas in which further study is indicated. The individual program will take into account the candidate's age, culture, past studies and experience. The Ecclesiastical Delegate arranges for the assessment interview and advises the sponsoring bishop.

B.   The Bibliography is a list of theological books compiled by the Ecclesiastical Delegate's theological consultors and is designed to include all topics on the Assessment Instrument. In the assessment interview the assessors can review with the petitioner the bibliography and highlight titles which may involve reading sections of various books or the books in their entirety which pertain to the needs. It is not presumed that anyone will study the entire bibliography. The bibliography would indicate where such books would be available. The sponsoring bishop may appoint a learned priest to guide the petitioner's study. It is understood that the time required for study depends upon the petitioner's need and available time.

C. <u>The Certification Examination</u> is the conclusion of the process and is intended to assure the sponsoring bishop that the petitioner is theologically qualified for ordination as a Catholic priest. This exam may be taken as soon as consent to the dossier is received from the Congregation for the Doctrine of the Faith and the petitioner is prepared. The exam is prepared by the designated consultors. The petitioner should understand that he is responsible for the entire syllabus.

<u>The Certification Examination</u> consists of two parts. A written exam will be administered through the office of the sponsoring bishop in the petitioner's place of residence. After the completed exam is read by the theological consultors, a date is arranged for the oral portion of this final exam and the petitioner meets with the team. Arrangements for the examination are made by the Ecclesiastical Delegate in consultation with the sponsoring bishop.

It is presumed that the sponsoring bishop will pay expenses incurred by the Assessment and the Certification Examination (i.e., travel, lodging, photo copying, etc.) However, other suitable arrangements can be made with the candidate.

8. Priestly Formation—Spiritual

The sponsoring bishop shall appoint a capable priest to meet regularly with the petitioner. This priest would serve as a formation director and a source of support for the petitioner. The spiritual formation programme would correspond to the one outlined by the Canadian Conference of Catholic Bishops in its <u>Programme for Priestly Formation.</u>

9.   At some time during the process it is expected that plans would be made to receive the petitioner into full communion and to confirm him. This should be done as soon as possible and practicable.

The Apostolic See expects that a petitioner should experience full communion for one year before he would be ordained. The sponsoring bishop may petition the Congregation through the Ecclesiastical Delegate for a reduction of this time after a <u>Rescript</u> is issued and the Certification Examination is completed, if he has sufficient pastoral reasons for doing so.

10. When a <u>Rescript</u> permitting ordination is received from the Congregation for the Doctrine of the Faith, the Ecclesiastical Delegate communicates this fact to the petitioner's sponsoring bishop. When the petitioner has satisfactorily completed the Certification Examination and any other requirements imposed by the sponsoring bishop are met, the petitioner may be ordained deacon, then priest by his bishop. He is incardinated in the usual manner.

11. The sponsoring bishop shall make suitable provisions for registration of the newly-ordained cleric in the diocesan pension plan, and shall determine that suitable arrangements have been made for the support of the cleric's wife and family in the event of the priest's subsequent death or disability.

June 1991

FREDERICK J. LUHMANN

Pastoral Guidelines for Churches in the Case of Clergy Moving from One Communion to the Other

I. ORDAINED MINISTRY IN THE LIFE OF THE CHURCH

1. In Canada over the past few years there have been instances of Anglican or Roman Catholic clergy joining the other church and wishing to exercise an ordained ministry. Sometimes there have been unfortunate consequences, resulting in uncertainty and confusion among members of both churches. The individuals concerned are motivated by deep personal reasons but people do not always understand what has happened or why. We hope that such transitions might not be occasions of triumphalism but will take place in ways appropriate to a relationship between two churches which today receive each other as sister churches in real but imperfect communion. For this reason, it will be helpful for both churches in such cases to deal with each other openly and in a spirit of collaboration and by so doing give a sign of mutual respect to the world.

2. For a quarter of a century, Anglicans and Roman Catholics have been engaged "in a serious dialogue which, founded on the gospels and on the ancient traditions, may lead to that unity in truth, for which Christ prayed." (Common Declaration of Pope Paul VI and Archbishop Michael Ramsey, 1966). One of the fruits of that dialogue has been a growing appreciation of the ministry exercised in the other church. In the Agreed Statement on Ministry and Ordination (Windsor, 1973), the Anglican-Roman

119

Catholic International Commission claims to have reached consensus on essential matters related to the nature of ordained ministry and its role in the life of the Church. It is in this context, far removed from the more polemical approach which often marred earlier relationships, that the question of the movement of persons in the ordained ministry from one church to the other should be approached.

3. Another important element in our dealing with the persons seeking admission to the ordained ministry within the other church might be a profound respect for the conscience of those whose pilgrimage of faith has made such a move seem desirable and necessary to them. The intention of these guidelines is a pastoral one, to ensure that the procedures followed are a help and not a hindrance to individuals in clarifying the motivation and implications of their movement into the communion of the other church. It is also important to keep in mind the needs and concerns of the church communities which are involved and in which they will eventually serve.

4. We wish to ensure that such occasions are not disruptive of our growing ecumenical relationship. We are convinced that sensitivity to the rights of both individuals and particular churches will not conflict with the growing appreciation of the real but imperfect communion which already exists between our churches.

5. There are several important reasons why pastoral guidelines are appropriate for dealing with cases of clergy moving from one communion to the other:

a) In both communions the ordained ministry is a public office, representing a focus of leadership and unity within the church. When an individual decides to move into communion with another church it cannot avoid coming to the attention of the wider community and giving rise to questions and concerns regarding the relationship between the two churches involved.

b) Ordained ministry is carried out within the context of a worshiping and serving community which needs a pastor who understands it. Guidelines for the movement of ordained persons from communion with one church into communion with the other should ensure that the person concerned is given the opportunity to become familiar with the rites and ethos of the receiving community.

c) It is important for both the applicant and the church to discern if those in pastoral leadership have the vocation and qualities appropriate to the exercise of ordained ministry. This is why both churches have procedures to be followed before admitting candidates into the exercise of ordained ministry, and there are particular policies regarding the admission of persons ordained in another church. These guidelines presuppose that such regulations are understood and followed.

d) Persons leaving one church for the other need to be aware of the ecumenical dialogue between us, which aims at nothing less than the restoration of full communion between sister churches. Any move from one to the other ought to be motivated primarily by a love for the new church, not by frustration or anger, and the bishop receiving such a person should encourage a healthy respect for the former church and for our continuing search for reconciliation and understanding.

II.   ASSISTING APPLICANTS IN DISCERNMENT OF VOCATION

A.   Initial Approach

6.   From a theological perspective baptism precedes ordination. That is, church membership is prior to the seeking of ordained ministry in the church of which one is a member. Further, commitment to the doctrine and practice of the receiving church must be broader than a single issue which may appear to have motivated the change. Although it is difficult to discern among the complexity of human motivations, it is important to attend to the differences between opportunism and spiritual growth. Applicants will also need to become used to the similarities and differences which characterize the two churches. It may, therefore, be appropriate for them to spend two or three years as a practicing member of the receiving church and have the opportunity of learning its ethos before either ordination or reception into ordained ministry.

7.   Before leaving one church for another it would be helpful to bring closure to the earlier relationship. Among other things, the person should be encouraged to contact the former bishop and be informed that the

122

receiving bishop will want to talk with the former bishop.

8.   In both churches there are procedures for helping individuals discern their vocation, and to identify right intention and the possession of the spiritual, moral, personal and social qualities integral to the exercise of ordained ministry.   Applicants who have been ordained in the other church should be asked to give careful consideration to: a) their commitment to the receiving church, b) signs of vocation specific to that church, and c) for those entering the Roman Catholic Church, the significance of the link between celibacy and the priesthood.

The Call to Celibacy or Marriage

9.   Both churches acknowledge that marriage, celibacy and priesthood are all gifts of God. There is, however, a difference of approach between the two churches in the link recognized between celibacy and priesthood.

    a)   A married priest moving from the Anglican tradition into the Roman Catholic Church needs to be aware that the majority of his colleagues in the presbyterium will be celibate and that the Roman Catholic Church is committed to the principle of linking celibacy and priesthood. Under certain circumstances permission can be granted for married men to be ordained, but the basic model is renunciation of marriage for the sake of the Kingdom.

b) In the case of someone coming to the Anglican Church from the Roman Catholic tradition, the Anglican bishop will want to discern that the applicant is not making the change solely out of a desire for marriage. He will also want to be sure that any marriage that exists is firmly established before ordination or reception into ordained ministry. It should also be noted that while the Anglican tradition recognizes that some may discern a call to celibacy this is not a qualification for ordained ministry.

Signs of Vocation

a) Subjective Perception

10. An exploration of the applicant's own sense of vocation should include such matters as: a) a brief autobiographical statement including a description of the persons, events, and institutions which have shaped the applicant's development in either a positive or negative manner; b) a history of the candidate's vocational and spiritual development; c) an appraisal of the candidate's personal and professional strengths; d) an assessment of the applicant's relationship to the church at this stage of spiritual and emotional development; e) a description of the applicant's personal and vocational goals; f) the applicant's perception of authority and the way the applicant sees himself exercising it; g) motivation or desire for change at the present state of personal and vocational development; h) hopes and dreams for the future.

b)   Authority's Assessment

11.   In both our traditions it is the bishop who carries ultimate responsibility, upon informed recommendation, for making an assessment of the applicant's suitability for ordination. Both churches also have structures to help the bishop make such an informed decision: the presbyterium or council of priests, the seminary team, the Advisory Committee on Postulants for Ordination, etc. Appropriate assessment procedures should be followed. It may be important to explore attitudes toward authority and colleagues in ministry. It is important that underlying differences with the position of the former church on such matters as celibacy or the ordination of women do not reflect negative attitudes toward authority which could make it difficult for the person to adjust to life in the new church.

c)   Community Discernment

12.   Although traditions see the ordained ministry as having a distinctive role which is not simply "an extension of the common Christian priesthood but belongs to another realm of the gifts of the Spirit" (Ministry and Ordination, para. A. 13), they would also agree that the priesthood is exercised in and for the sake of Christian community. As part of his ministry of oversight the bishop has a particular obligation to ensure that the community is served by clergy who understand its ethos and are sensitive to its needs. For this reason it is important for lay members of the church to be involved in the assessment of the candidate's capacity to function as an ordained minister in the new context according to the disciplines of the respective churches.

B.   Communication Between Bishops

13.   The movement of clergy between our churches implies a responsibility on the part of the church as well as the individual. Anglican and Roman Catholic bishops in Canada have been in dialogue for a considerable time and sufficient mutual confidence has been built up so that they should be in contact as early as possible when one or other is approached by clergy wanting to move from one church to the other. Questions to be discussed include: 1) the personality of the candidate; 2) the authenticity of the candidate's earlier calling to ordained ministry and in the case of one leaving the Roman Catholic Church, his vocation to the celibate life; 3) the candidate's capacity as a pastor in the community that is being left; and 4) any other information that will be of assistance to both the individual and the receiving church.

14.   The financial situation of the candidate should be part of the conversation between the bishops. What, for example, does a person do during the waiting period? The need could be especially acute if the individual concerned is married and has a family.

15.   It may also be necessary for the two bishops to discuss the question of publicity and media interest in the movement of a particular priest. A competitive approach does not accurately reflect the relationship which our two churches now enjoy. Instead, cooperation between the respective bishops can be a living demonstration of the search for unity and reconciliation in which both churches are currently engaged. Consideration should be given to a joint announcement or to a coordinated response.

Applicants themselves should be discouraged from making statements.

III. FOLLOWING APPROPRIATE PROCEDURES

16. Bishops should be aware of the procedures applicable in the sister church for the reception of those ordained in another tradition. Guidelines should be shared where available and differences in procedure should be respected. Through dialogue, in an atmosphere of mutual regard and respect the reasons behind the particular requirements can be clarified and their intention understood. As a result of this process, it is to be hoped that if there are any aspects of our respective procedures which could give rise to offense they will be modified insofar as the competence of the leadership of our respective churches is able to do so.

17. One area of difference is a disparity in practice regarding ordination or reordination. A bishop of the Roman Catholic Church will be required by its discipline to ordain a person ordained according to the rites of the Anglican Church. On the other hand, a priest lawfully ordained in the Roman Catholic Church would normally be received, rather than ordained, on admission into ordained ministry in the Anglican Church. This will continue to be a source of pain and misunderstanding as long as our two churches do not mutually recognize each other's ordinations. The recognition of each other's ministries and the restoration of full communion continues to be the objective of the dialogue being carried out by the Anglican-Roman Catholic International Commission and by a variety of regional and national dialogues.

IV.   PASTORAL SUPPORT FOR THOSE
IN TRANSITION

18.   Just as a newly ordained person needs time and support to become comfortable with life in the ordained ministry, this need should not be overlooked for the person in transition. Special consideration should be given to pastoral support during the first year or two after an individual has been ordained or received into ordained ministry in the other church. The bishop should appoint a capable team including a priest and some lay people who will meet regularly with the person concerned in order to serve as a source of support and provide continued formation in ordained ministry in the new church.

19.   Individual circumstances will call for flexibility. The nature and duration of the person's experience in the former church, as well as his understanding of the receiving church should be taken into account in the planning of early placements. For the common good, the person concerned should usually not be placed in the same area that was served in prior to the change. Such early service will often take place in a non-parish setting or as an assistant to the pastor of a parish to give the person an opportunity to adapt and better equip himself to serve the people of the church with which he has now identified.

20.   We are aware this document focuses primarily on those moving from priesthood in one church to the priesthood in the other. Other circumstances of transition can be envisioned, including the deacon or lay person who may feel called to seek priesthood in the other church. We believe that if the same principles of ecumenical and pastoral sensitivity are

applied these also can be occasions of growth and understanding.

21.   The Church is called to proclaim the reconciling love of God in Christ, to be a people among whom this love is manifested and the instrument through which salvation is offered to all. It is this priesthood of the whole Church which the ordained ministry seeks to serve. May God guide and nurture all men and women in their various ministries within the community of the faithful.

The gifts he gave were that some would be apostles, some prophets, some evangelists, some pastors and teachers, to equip the saints for the work of ministry, for building up the body of Christ, until all of us come to the unity of the faith and of the knowledge of the Son of God, to maturity, to the measure of the full stature of Christ. (Ephesians 4.11-13) (N.R.S.V.)

November 1991

ENGLAND and WALES

Fifteen years after the pastoral provision was approved for the United States, Pope John Paul II granted a comparable authority to England and Wales on June 2, 1995. The five archbishops of England and Wales announced the approval in a June 29 letter to the priests of England and Wales. The text of the letter follows:

Dear Father,

At the Low Week meeting of the bishops' conference, it was unanimously agreed to send the following message to all the priests of England and Wales:

At the present time the Catholic Church is welcoming into full communion a number of married clergymen of the Church of England, often together with their wives and in some cases their children. We, the bishops of England and Wales, are of one mind in our desire to welcome them.

Many of these clergy wish to be ordained priests in the Catholic Church. We are engaged in discerning God's will for each of them. We are convinced that their ministry will enrich the church.

With the full approval of the Holy See, arrangements will shortly be in place in this country for considering applications for the ordination to the priesthood of these former married Anglican clergy. Permission for each ordination has to be given by the Holy Father, but in these new circumstances the procedures leading to his decision have been entrusted to this bishops' conference.

The Holy Father has asked us to be generous. We are confident that you also will welcome and appreciate these new priests when, in due course, they begin to serve in different capacities in the life and mission of the church.

This message will shortly be included in diocesan pastoral letters to all the faithful. But at this important moment in our history and at the request of the bishops' conference, we want to send in advance to you, our priests, this special word of encouragement and explanation.

Much has been said in recent years about the movement of Anglicans into full communion with the Catholic Church. Clearly many such people have long sought to lead a Catholic life within the Church of England, and they have become convinced that only full, visible communion with the Catholic Church can ensure this. Clergymen among them, whether married or single, have meantime faithfully observed the disciplines of the Church of England, and this has tested their sense of vocation to ministry.

Out of respect for that ministry, we have set in motion the process of discernment necessary for them to go forward to ordination to the priesthood. Where this process concerns married men, it will mean quite new responsibilities for our bishops' conference. This means that in the near future married priests will take their place in the presbyterate of many of our dioceses. They will not be the first examples of this, as in the last few years there have already been several cases. Yet the presence of these married priests, as distinct from the steadily increasing number of married

131

deacons, undoubtedly does raise a number of sensitive issues.

There may be some people who think of this development as the beginning of a process of change affecting the church's discipline of celibacy. We do not see it this way. The special permissions needed in these cases are by way of exception from the general practice of the Western church of accepting only single men for priesthood. Each permission is reserved to the Holy Father and is granted out of recognition of the particular journey of faith into full communion. It is a journey which has included the discernment and reception of orders within a church with which we share much and which, of course, permits the marriage of its clergy. But each candidate has to accept the general norm of celibacy and will not be free to marry again. It is to be understood that the special procedures involving the bishops' conference in the admission of former married Anglican clergy to the priesthood will be operative for four years only.

These men, with their wives and families, are in quite a different situation from that of married laymen or married deacons within the Catholic Church who may have a desire for ordination to the priesthood. In our consideration of this question, we have been aware also of the situation of those ordained priests who have left their priestly ministry and are now married. We recognize that when married former Anglicans are admitted to the priesthood, the pain of difficult decisions and losses will be reawakened in those priests who left the priesthood to marry. We hope that you will help those who left the priesthood to marry with your friendship, understanding and support.

In fact, the circumstances of those who have left the exercise of their priestly ministry in the Catholic Church are not the same as those of the married former clergy of the Church of England. We have a duty to respect and support these latter in their fidelity to the marriage promises to which they have committed themselves prior to their asking to become Catholic priests. In practice these two vocations, marriage and priesthood, are probably not easy to hold together for either spouse, so this again calls for understanding and support.

A married priest, with wife and family, needs a different level of financial support from that of his celibate colleagues. Many of these men who are now seeking full communion are making startling sacrifices. They are not expecting a large income. Yet we must be realistic and imaginative in the arrangements we make. We ask that you cooperate generously in the proposals which will be suggested and discussed with you when the time arises.

Your welcome will mean much to these new priests. The experience of a diocesan presbyterate is one of the great strengths of the priesthood in the Catholic Church. We are sure that our presbyterate will in fact be strengthened and enriched by its new members. They will be working in many different capacities, but certainly not exclusively parochial duties and responsibilities. As you probably know, they will not be given the full canonical status of a parish priest at the present time.

We would also like you to know that
our discussions of these matters with the Holy
See over the last few years have been most
constructive and encouraging. For us it has
been a positive experience of cooperation in
which our judgment has been sought and
trusted. We are grateful for this. The Holy
Father himself has been personally involved
and, seeming to sense in this an important
historical moment, has shown exceptional
generosity to those earnestly seeking life in the
Catholic Church.

We commend these important
developments to your earnest prayers that we
may all have the guidance of the Holy Spirit in
these developments of such importance to our
church. Our duty, readily undertaken, is to
pass on to you this encouragement and
exhortation from the Holy Father. Be
generous. We are confident that in being so
we shall all be enriched.

Cardinal George Basil Hume
Archbishop of Westminster

Archbishop Derek Worlock
Archbishop of Liverpool

Archbishop Michael Bowen
Archbishop of Southwark

Archbishop Maurice Couve de Murville
Archbishop of Birmingham

Archbishop John Alysius Ward
Archbishop of Cardiff

The letter of the bishops reflects a refreshing openness in announcing the introduction of the pastoral provision. The bishops immediately inform and engage as colleagues in a common endeavor each priest in England and Wales. They commit themselves, shortly, to issue a pastoral letter to all of the faithful. Introduction of the pastoral provision is recognized for what it is — a major event which will affect the life and practice of the entire Church.

The bishops' letter indicates: "At the present time the Catholic Church is welcoming into full communion a number of married clergymen of the Church of England . . . " but the letter gives no explanation as to the reason for the phenomenon. Perhaps no reason was needed for the intended readers of the letter in England and Wales who were aware of the dynamics underlying the movement of the clergymen from one church to the other. However, readers of the letter who are unfamiliar with the background of events may be excused if they ask: "Why did so many Anglican clergymen, married or single, each enter upon a 'particular journey of faith into full communion' at that time?"

Cause-effect relationships are very difficult to establish even in the most controlled scientific studies. It would be precarious, therefore, to posit such a relationship between the actions of individual Anglican clergymen and the events which were taking place within the Church of England in the period of time immediately preceding the bishops' letter. It is possible, however, to note certain similarities to events which took place during the 1970's within the Episcopal Church in the United States before the initiation of the pastoral provision of 1980.

The General Synod, the legislative body of the Church of England, voted to allow the ordination of women priests on November 11, 1992. This vote was enacted into law as the Priests (Ordination of Women) Measure 1993 with an effective date of February 22, 1994. The first women were ordained under the act at Bristol Cathedral in 1994. While the "Measure," as it is called, provided that women might be ordained as priests, it left discretion to individual bishops on the matter. The Measure, also, explicitly precluded the consecration of women as bishops. Reportedly more than 470 male clergy left the Anglican priesthood as a result of the Act of Ministry. The most notable example of such a departure is discussed elsewhere. In July 2000 the General Synod meeting at York voted overwhelmingly to begin "further theological study" on the episcopate over the next two years in preparation for future debate concerning the consecration of women as bishops.[53]

Early in the letter the bishops explicitly welcome the wives and children of the married clergymen who seek full communion and Catholic priesthood. The bishops note that they are convinced the church will be enriched by the ministry of these married converts and future priests. The unanimous enthusiasm of the bishops arises from the request of the Holy Father who personally asked them to be generous in receiving these married former Anglican clergymen, together with their families, into full communion with the Catholic Church and, in due course, into the Catholic priesthood.

Despite the Holy Father's request for generosity, the letter demonstrates that in a number of areas the pastoral provision for England and Wales will be encumbered by the same restrictions which apply to the United States and Canada: 1. While married candidates will be accepted for ordination, each must accept the general norm of celibacy for the Catholic Church in the West and may not remarry in the event of widowhood. 2. Married priests will not be given the full canonical status of parish priests. 3. Each permission for ordination is reserved to the Holy Father. Also, the pastoral provision was approved for four years only.

One sentence in the letter strikes a discordant and not easily understood note. In speaking of the admission of married former Anglican clergy to the Catholic priesthood, the letter reads: "These men, with their wives and families, are in quite a different situation from that of married laymen or married deacons within the Catholic Church who may have a desire for ordination to the priesthood."

The situation of the convert clergy who come into full communion with the Catholic Church certainly is different from that of married laymen or deacons who always have been Catholics. The difference is that the latter have been born into the Catholic Church, believed in and followed the teachings of the Church for their entire lives, been married with a sacrament of the Church, and raised their families according to the teachings of the Catholic Church. Additionally, the permanent deacons have been called from the community, have been trained in service to the People of God, have made a lifetime commitment to the Church, and have received a sacred order one step removed from the priesthood. Indeed, they are different from married former Anglican clergy who seek to be ordained as priests of the Catholic Church. It is unclear, however, why their differences should disqualify them in their desire to be ordained to the Catholic priesthood.

The Statutes

Statutes prepared by the English and Welsh bishops for admitting married former clergymen of the Church of England to the Roman Catholic priesthood were approved by Pope John Paul II June 2 and announced in London June 30, 1995. The statutes took effect on July 2 and are to remain in force for the next four years. "Three bishops shall be nominated by the bishops' conference as the commission for dealing with requests for ordination from married former Anglican clergy," according to the statutes. Among points the commission will evaluate are "the stability of the marriage and evidence of the support of the wife for the ordination and priestly ministry of her husband." Also related to the candidate's suitability is his openness "to the theological and pastoral perspectives of the Catholic Church as taught by the Second Vatican Council." The statutes say that the candidate's period of preparation for priesthood normally will be two years. Also discussed in the statutes are cases to be referred to Rome, the pastoral role of the married priests and the ordination itself. The statutes follow.

Introduction

1.1 These statutes are drawn up by the Bishops' Conference of England and Wales in the light of the directives given by the Congregation for the Doctrine of the Faith (cf. Letter to Cardinal Hume of Dec. 22, 1994, DF 142/93). They come into effect one month after receiving approval from the Holy See and shall remain in force for a period of four years from that date.

1.2 These statutes take account of the particular situation that has arisen in England since the Decision of the Synod of the Church of England to ordain women to the priesthood. A considerable number of former Anglican clergy, both single and married, have been or are in the process of being received into full communion in the Catholic Church, and many of them wish to be ordained as priests in the Catholic Church. In responding to these requests a number of factors have to be born in mind, including the manner in which these clergy can best serve the people of God in different dioceses and the ways in which adequate financial support can be provided

1.3 The bishops' conference will keep this situation under constant review during the next four years.

1.4 The bishops' conference reaffirms its commitment to the law of celibacy in the Latin church.

The Commission

2.1 Three bishops shall be nominated by the bishops' conference to serve as the commission for dealing with requests for ordination from married former Anglican clergy.

2.2 The president of the commission approved by the Holy See is to act as the ecclesiastical delegate for relations with the Holy See.

Procedure

3.1 Once the candidate has been received into full communion, the diocesan bishop may receive a petition for admission to orders and forward it to the commission. In doing so the bishop will provide the necessary documentation (cf. enclosures). In addition he will provide:
- His *votum* on the opportuneness of his admission and incardination into the diocese.
- His proposals for the program of preparation to be followed by the candidate.
- The pastoral duties to be entrusted to the candidate after ordination.

3.2 In coming to its decisions the commission will take note of the following:

a) Suitability of Candidate
i) The stability of the marriage and evidence of the support of the wife for the ordination and priestly ministry of her husband.
ii) The openness of the candidate to the theological and pastoral perspectives of the Catholic Church as taught by the Second Vatican Council.
iii) The capacity and readiness of the candidate to be incorporated into the diocesan presbyterate.
iv) The willingness of the candidate to support the norm of celibacy for the clergy in the Latin church.

b) *Opportuneness of Admission and Incardination*

i) The particular circumstances pertaining in the diocese, such as its pastoral needs, history and social circumstances.

ii) The number of such cases already admitted in the diocese.

c) *Studies and Formation*

i) In the light of previous academic studies and pastoral experience, studies must be undertaken which will ensure, in particular, competence in the following areas: dogmatic theology, ecclesiology, moral theology, canon law, sacramental practice.

ii) The period of preparation will normally be of two years duration after reception into full communion.

d) *Pastoral Duties*

i) In general, married priests shall not be assigned to the "ordinary care of souls." They are to be entrusted, as a rule, with administration, social or educational work where the ordinary judges that work to be compatible with priestly ordination.

ii) When, in particular circumstances, it is judged necessary by the ordinary to meet the pastoral and spiritual needs of the people, married priests may give assistance in and carry out the full range of priestly duties.

iii) In no case may married priests have all the responsibilities which fall to those who hold the office of parish priest.

e) Time and Manner of Ordination

i) All candidates are to be ordained absolutely, according to the teaching and constant practice of the church in this regard.

ii) All candidates are dispensed from receiving the ministries of lector and acolyte.

iii) After the appropriate preparation and formal discernment, candidates shall receive ordination to the diaconate and ordination to the priesthood, following the common law of the church regarding interstices.

iv) The liturgical rite of the Roman Pontifical shall be followed, with the inclusion —before the examination of the candidate in the rite of ordination to the diaconate — of a prayer of thanksgiving for the ministry exercised in the Anglican Communion.

3.3 When the examination of the petition has been concluded, the commission shall give its *votum* on the case, indicating affirmative (with eventual conditions attached), negative or *casus examini Sanctae Sedis subiciatur.* If the decision is negative, the sponsoring bishop is free to appeal to the Holy See (via the Congregation for the Doctrine of the Faith).

3.4 The commission shall refer to the Congregation for the Doctrine of the Faith the following cases:

a) Those of former Anglican bishops who ask for some form of recognition of their previous episcopal status.

b) Those which involve a request for ordination *sub condicione.*

c) Those of any groups who wish corporate reconciliation.

3.5 For those who have exercised episcopal ministry within the Anglican Communion, out of consideration for their previous dignity, the competent authority (the commission or the Congregation for the Doctrine of the Faith) shall judge the appropriateness of proposing to the Holy Father the concession of priestly ordination alone.

3.6 The liturgical formulas in those cases in which priestly ordination alone is conferred and in cases of ordination *sub condicione* shall be decided beforehand by the Holy See.

3.7 In cases reserved to the Holy See, the commission shall transmit all the documentation to the Congregation for the Doctrine of the Faith, which will add its own recommendation.

Reference to the Holy See

4.1 The cases decided by the commission shall be presented by its president to the Holy Father through the Congregation for the Doctrine of the Faith which will add its *visum*.

4.2 The president of the commission shall present a report to the Congregation for the Doctrine of the Faith at the end of every year on the cases received and decided as well as on the general situation.

These statutes were approved by Pope John Paul II on June 2, 1995.

The Statues differ in some details from the processes which have been discussed for the United States and Canada. The Introduction clearly establishes a connection between the Statutes and the decision of the Church of England to ordain women to the priesthood. The pastoral provision in the United States did not acknowledge such a connection to the ordination of women by the Episcopal Church.

A second difference from the United States is that three bishops are named to form a commission(2.1) for the administration of the Statutes. The commission president is to serve as the ecclesiastical delegate for relations with the Holy See.

The Statutes do not provide a list of particular steps to be followed in the process, but indicate that a sponsoring bishop is to provide necessary documentation based on enclosures which apparently were transmitted with the Statutes. The sponsoring bishop also is requested to provide information to the commission concerning the duties which the candidate will undertake after ordination. The period of preparation after reception into full communion is set at two years. The normal time period for the United States is one year, but a sponsoring bishop may request from the Congregation for the Doctrine of the Faith permission to ordain in a shorter period.

The Statutes include an explicit statement regarding the limitation on the ministry of married priests which is the same as the limitation for the United States and Canada. The processes of the latter countries, however, do not explicitly mention the limitation. Section 3.2 d) iii states: "In no case may married priests have all the responsibilities which fall to those who hold the office of parish priest." Section 3.4 identifies special cases which shall be referred to the Congregation for the Doctrine of the Faith, including cases of former Anglican bishops who ask for some form of recognition of their previous episcopal status.

The Statutes conclude with a requirement that the commission present an annual report to the Congregation for the Doctrine of the Faith on cases received and decided and on the general situation. Such reports do not appear to be in the public domain.

As of the end of 1999 the Catholic Bishops' Conference of England and Wales confirmed that 110 married former Anglican clergy had been ordained Catholic priests for dioceses in England and Wales. The conference also indicated that the Statutes had been extended for a further three years beyond the original expiration date of July 1999.[54]

Among the married convert Anglican clergy ordained as Catholic priests was the former Most Reverend Graham Leonard, retired Anglican bishop of London, the third-ranking see in the Church of England. In an interview with England's National Catholic Register, the former Anglican Bishop explained his decision to seek full communion with the Catholic Church as follows: "For me, the vote over women was the trigger, as it were. After that went through, I realized quite clearly that I had to seek communion with the See of Peter as the proper thing to do if I was going to live as a Catholic. I put my situation into Cardinal Hume's hands and that of Rome and I took what came out."[55]

What came out was that the Holy See approved his ordination to the Catholic priesthood *sub condicione.* Pope Leo XIII's Papal Bull, *Apostolicae Curae,* of 1896 which declared Anglican orders "absolutely null and utterly void" evidently did not present an impediment to the conditional ordination of former Bishop Leonard as a Catholic priest in 1995. Contrary to the adamant assertion of Leo XIII that Anglican orders under no circumstances could be considered valid, the conditional ordination of The Reverend Leonard suggested the possibility that the ordination in the Church of England which he had previously received, in fact, might have been valid.

OTHER CASES

The pastoral provisions of the United States, Canada, England and Wales each share the following common characteristics. First, the National Conference of Catholic Bishops in each country submitted a formal request to the Holy See for approval to ordain to the Catholic priesthood married former clergy of the Anglican tradition. Second, the Holy See granted each request under essentially the same conditions. Third, an ecclesiastical delegate — or in the case of England and Wales a committee of bishops whose president served as the ecclesiastical delegate — was named as the official liaison with the Holy See for all matters related to the pastoral provision. Fourth, paragraph 42 of Pope Paul VI's encyclical *Sacerdotalis caelibatus* is cited in support of the pastoral provisions. That paragraph reads:

> n.42 In virtue of the fundamental norm of the government of the Catholic Church, to which We alluded above, while on the one hand, the law requiring a freely chosen and perpetual celibacy of those who are admitted to Holy Orders remains unchanged, on the other hand, a study may be allowed of the particular circumstances of married sacred ministers of Churches of other Christian communities separated from the Catholic communion, and of the possibility of admitting to priestly functions those who desire to adhere to the fullness of this communion and to continue to exercise the sacred ministry. The circumstances must be such, however, as not to prejudice the existing discipline regarding celibacy.

The wording of the encyclical is that "a study may be allowed . . . " There is no evidence that a study of any nature was ever conducted between 1967, the date of the encyclical, and 1980, the date of the first pastoral provision. Nor is there any indication that a study of any nature has been done of the implementation of the pastoral provisions in effect until this date.

Aside from the notion that a study should be conducted before any action might be taken, there is another key idea expressed by Pope Paul VI, namely that the study extend to the "particular circumstances of married sacred ministers of Churches of other Christian communities . . ." The encyclical did not single out the sacred ministers of any particular Christian Church for study. Rather, it spoke of "other Christian communities" without any limitation.

As the years passed following the issuance of the encyclical, the study referred to by Pope Paul VI was not conducted. However, clergy of the Episcopal Church in the United States, and later of the Anglican Churches of Canada, England and Wales, who wished to enter into full communion with the Catholic Church and to be ordained as Catholic priests, initiated contact with the Conference of Catholic Bishops for their respective countries. Each Conference of Catholic Bishops, in turn, sought and received from the Holy See a pastoral provision specific to a particular jurisdiction.

Married former clergy of the Episcopal and Anglican Churches have constituted the most notable groups to come into full communion with the Catholic Church and to be ordained as Catholic priests. However, they are not the only married former clergy of other Christian Churches who have come into full communion and been ordained as Catholic priests.

147

Reflecting on the pastoral provision for the United States, Fichter offered the following comment:

> One may well wonder why such an elaborate protocol has grown up around a procedure that ought to be relatively simple. There was really no need for a collective request by the U.S. Bishops, nor for a litany of "new" directions from Rome in response. In the formal transaction to bring a minister — even a married man — from another Church into the Catholic clergy, any diocesan Ordinary may simply request that the Holy Father grant a rescript in each particular case. Apparently, no U.S. Bishop felt courageous to "set the precedent" for this country. [56]

Witness to the truth of Fichter's assessment is the fact that in recent years a number of married former clergy of Christian Churches that are not included in the pastoral provisions have been received into full communion with the Catholic Church and have been ordained as Catholic priests. With the exception of the first example noted below, it appears that in each case a local Ordinary did as Fichter indicated and made a direct request to the Holy See for a rescript without channeling the request through Cardinal Law.

Since there is no national clearinghouse responsible to process such requests or retain information about them, there are no accurate national data on the total number of priests who have been ordained in this manner. However, it is evident that applicants from other Christian Churches have followed a similar, if not identical, process and been ordained under the same restraints as the Episcopal priests included under the original intent of the pastoral provision.

Several examples follow of married priests who formerly were sacred ministers in the Methodist, Presbyterian and Lutheran Churches. The examples do not suggest that these are the only married priests from each of these denominations or that there are not married priests from other Christian Churches.

In the fall of 1967 John Giles entered Candler School of Theology at Emory University to begin a course of studies that led in 1971 to his ordination as an Elder in the Florida Conference of the United Methodist Church and to a pastorate at Redlands Community Church in Homestead, Florida. While stationed at Homestead, The Reverend Giles developed a friendship with Father John Gubbins and began to admire the Catholic Faith. Three years later, while serving as "Minister in and to Society," The Reverend Giles met and married a young social worker named Carol Turner. Over time, the family of John and Carol grew to include two sons, David Paul and Michael Philip.

Continued personal study, involvement in interfaith ministry, and deepening personal friendships drew The Reverend Giles increasingly toward the Catholic Faith. In June 1982 he accepted an appointment with the Moss Bluff United Methodist Church in Lake Charles, Louisiana. His next door neighbor, soon to become family friend, was Monsignor Joseph Bourque, pastor of Saint Theodore Catholic Church. In that same period as a result of working together on the Louisiana Interchurch Conference, The Reverend Giles developed a close relationship with Bishop Jude Speyer, the Catholic Bishop of the Lake Charles Diocese.

In April 1984, The Reverend Giles asked Monsignor Bourque the question that had been on his mind for some time: "Can I become a Catholic priest?" Monsignor Bourque brought the question to Bishop Speyer who inquired of the

Holy See whether a married Methodist Minister who entered the Catholic Church might be ordained as a Catholic priest. The Holy See responded affirmatively and The Reverend Giles entered upon the same path of preparation for the priesthood as did Episcopalian applicants under the pastoral provision.

On May 23, 1985, John and Carol, together with their children, were received into "full communion" with the Catholic Church. That same year Bishop Speyer petitioned the Holy See for a rescript to permit the ordination of John Giles as a Catholic priest. Two years later the rescript was granted on April 30, 1987. In October, John was ordained a Deacon and on December 19, 1987 Bishop Jude Speyer ordained him in the Cathedral of the Immaculate Conception as a priest of the Lake Charles Diocese.

Following a number of other assignments, Father Giles received an appointment from Bishop Speyer to become Associate Pastor of Our Lady Queen of Heaven parish where he presently serves. Carol served for a number of years as the Director of the Office of Marriage and Family Ministries in the Diocese before accepting the position of Executive Director of Friends of Families, an ecumenical agency that works to provide service and assistance to homeless families.

Ten years after ordination to the priesthood Father Giles wrote of his family in these words:

> Carol has been my partner in life AND ministry throughout our life together. We are sounding boards for each other. We are support and encouragement for each other. It is the quality of our communication and sharing that has made my experience of living and of being a Catholic priest so wonderful. She is a source of

inspiration and strength for me. Our sons, David, who is eighteen, and Michael, who is fifteen, have grown up with me as a priest and have been a part of that not only in household conversations but also serving at the altar with me and other priests . . .

Sometimes I hear that being married makes it difficult to function as a priest. That has not been my experience. Far from pulling me away from service in the Church and to the people of God, my family has been a source of renewal and strength for me . . .

I believe that the presence and love of my family enables me to function at the highest level possible for me. It is because of the love, support, and presence of my family that I am empowered to be compassionate and understanding and to proclaim the Good News.[57]

Another former Methodist minister came to the Catholic priesthood in a different manner. In July 1996 Father Scott Medlock was ordained for the Archdiocese of Anchorage, Alaska. Father Medlock's path to the priesthood began as an undergraduate at Notre Dame University. Although a Methodist, Scott became interested in the Catholic Church. After marrying a Catholic, Maria Elena, Scott attended mass with her and raised their three children as Catholics. Meanwhile, he become a Methodist minister for nine years before personally entering the Catholic Church. In his search to find a bishop who would sponsor his candidacy for the priesthood, Scott moved his family in 1992 to Anchorage where Archbishop Francis T. Hurley agreed to sponsor him. While waiting to hear the response of the Holy See to his petition, Scott worked for the archdiocese. At his ordination Father Medlock was able to say: "I've been wholly embraced by the people of the archdiocese and the priests of the archdiocese."[58]

Several months after the ordination of Father Medlock, a former minister of another religious tradition was ordained for the Archdiocese of Portland. On November 30, 1996, Slider Steurnol, a 53-year-old, former Presbyterian minister, husband, and father of three ended an 11-year journey of faith that began when he attended a retreat at a Trappist abbey in Oregon. "I had reached a plateau in my life where I was hungry for God," he said. "I felt the wellspring of my spiritual life was dry. I came back from that retreat refreshed." [59]

In 1999 two married former Lutheran ministers were ordained as Catholic priests, one for the diocese of Austin, Texas, and the other for the Archdiocese of St. Paul and Minneapolis, Minnesota.

On July 10, 1999, Bishop John Mc Carthy ordained Father Larry Heimsoth as a Catholic priest for the diocese of Austin, Texas. Father Heimsoth, 54 at the time of his ordination, formerly was a Lutheran minister. He and his wife, Beverly, first entertained the idea of becoming Catholic two decades before they finally entered the Catholic Church in 1996. By that time their children had grown and lived independently. Although not covered by the pastoral provision, for about three years Father Heimsoth prepared for the priesthood in much the same manner as pastoral provision candidates.

At the time of his ordination Father Heimsoth said that "I've been prepared all my life for this. There's now a congruence between what I believe and what I'm doing."[60]

A second ordination of a former Lutheran minister took place far north of Texas in the December cold of the Archdiocese of St. Paul and Minneapolis. The ordinand was Father Lawrence Blake, husband and father of three children. At his ordination by Archbishop Harry Flynn on December 12, 1999, Father Blake became the first married priest in the 148-year history of the archdiocese. The 47-year-old Father Blake indicated that "For some time now, the focus of my spiritual journey has been the Eucharist as the center and source of our Christian faith."[61]

On August 12, 2000, another diocese far to the south celebrated the ordination of its first married priest. On that day, Father James McLelland, 53, who had served for twenty-two years as a minister in the United Methodist Church, became the first married priest of the Diocese of Shreveport, Louisiana. Father McLelland, the married father of two grown daughters and a grandfather, first met with Bishop William B. Friend in the fall of 1993. Later that same year Bishop Friend made initial contact with the Holy See to initiate the lengthy process preceding ordination.

In 1994, The Reverend McLelland took early retirement from the United Methodist Church and became Catholic. While awaiting final approval from the Holy See of his petition for ordination, he pursued additional theological studies. Following ordination to the priesthood, Father Mc Lelland was appointed by Bishop Friend to be the Apostolic Administrator of Saint Catherine of Siena parish in Shreveport. Father McLelland attributes the warm and accepting manner in which he and his family have been received by the parishioners at Saint Catherine's to the careful manner in which his predecessor prepared the members of the parish for the arrival of their married priest.[62]

On June 2, 2001, Bishop Joseph L. Imesch ordained to the priesthood a third married former Lutheran minister at the Cathedral of Saint Raymond in Joliet, Illinois. Father David Medow, 43, a graduate of Georgetown University and the Lutheran School of Theology in Chicago, served as a Lutheran minister from 1985 until he entered the Catholic Church on November 1, 1996. Father Medow and his wife, Jane who is a lifelong Catholic, have a son and a daughter. Father Medow received an assignment as assistant pastor at Saint Mary Immaculate parish in Plainfield where his wife teaches fifth grade at the parochial school.[63]

Although the discussion to this point has been limited to married Catholic priests in the United States, Canada, England and Wales, two additional cases are offered to show that married Catholic priests also exist in other countries.

In September 1993 the South African Diocesan News reported the ordination of Fr. David Evans which took place on August 14, 1993, at the Church of St. Theresa, Edenvale, Johannesburg, in the presence of his wife and three children, and many of his Anglican and Catholic friends. Fr. Evans was previously an ordained priest in the Anglican Church, and the process of his conversion started four years prior.[64]

In May 1998 the Archbishop of Castries, St.Lucia, Kelvin Felix ordained as a Catholic priest Dr. Leslie Lett, a married former Anglican priest. In attendance at the ceremony were Mrs. Phyllis Lett and their two children, Paul and Anna. Before his ordination Father Lett said he was deeply grateful for his years as an Anglican priest and that he found no conflict with what he believed formerly. Father Lett denied that his decision to join the Roman Catholic Church had anything to do with the fact that the Anglican Church in the Caribbean had recently decided to ordain women as priests. He stated that if the Catholic Church decided tomorrow to change its stance on the issue, he would have no problem accepting it.[65]

Since no database exists of all married priests, the preceding cases are offered simply as examples to establish an important point. In granting rescripts for the ordination to the Catholic priesthood of individual married former clergy of other Christian communions, the Holy See has shown an indisputable acceptance of the compatibility between married life and priestly ministry in the Western Church. The Holy Father requested the Bishops of England and Wales to be "generous" in responding to petitions from married former priests of the Church of England.

Yet, even as the Church has opened her arms to receive and ordain as priests married former clergy from other Christian communions, the Holy See repeatedly has expressed concern lest these exceptions might raise expectations that the general rule of celibacy as the norm for the Western Church would be relaxed. Pope Paul VI directed that any study about possible ordination of married former ministers of other Christian communions must be done in such a way as not to impact on the rule of celibacy. Pope John Paul II repeatedly has stated that the rule of clergy celibacy will not be changed. Each married pastoral provision priest is required to affirm a commitment to the general norm of celibacy and, if widowed, is prohibited from remarriage. Meanwhile, on June 6, 1997 the Holy See announced revised rules which make it easier for permanent deacons to remarry. Under the revised rules a widowed permanent deacon may receive a dispensation from the prohibition of Canon 1087 against remarriage for <u>any one</u> of the following three conditions: 1. The great and proven usefulness of the ministry of the deacon to the diocese to which he belongs, or 2. That he has children of such a tender age as to be in need of motherly care, or 3. That he has parents or parents-in-law who are elderly and in need of care.

My dear Irish mother would have been perplexed by the whole matter. With a shake of her head she would say, "Sure, and what is sauce for the goose is sauce for the gander."

2. EASTERN CATHOLIC CHURCHES

Perhaps the best way to establish the importance of the Eastern Catholic Churches is to begin with the words of the Second Vatican Council as found in the introductory paragraphs 1, 2, and 5 of the *Decree on the Catholic Churches of the Eastern Rite (Orientalium Ecclesiarum)*.

1. The Catholic Church holds in high esteem the institutions, liturgical rites, ecclesiastical traditions and the established standards of the Christian life of the Eastern Churches, for in them, distinguished as they are for their venerable antiquity, there remains conspicuous the tradition that has been handed down from the Apostles through the Fathers and that forms part of the divinely revealed and undivided heritage of the universal Church.

2. The Holy Catholic Church, which is the Mystical Body of Christ, is made up of the faithful who are organically united in the Holy Spirit by the same faith, the same sacraments and the same government and who, combining together into various groups which are held together by a hierarchy, form separate Churches or Rites. Between these there exists an admirable bond of union, such that the variety within the Church in no way harms its unity; rather it manifests it, for it is the mind of the Catholic Church that each individual Church or Rite should retain its traditions whole and entire and likewise that it should adapt its way of life to the different needs of time and place.

5. History, tradition and abundant ecclesiastical institutions bear outstanding witness to the great merit owing to the Eastern Churches by the universal Church. The Sacred Council, therefore, not only accords to this ecclesiastical and spiritual heritage the high regard which is its due and rightful praise, but also unhesitatingly looks on it as the heritage of the universal Church.[66]

These few paragraphs contain a wealth of material for the serious student of ecclesiology. For the rest of us, there is presented an inspiring call to appreciate and live up to the reality that: We are the Church, the Mystical Body of Christ, and each, one to the other, is organically united in the Holy Spirit and we believe deeply that variety within the Church in no way harms its unity; rather, it manifests it. "I am the vine and you are the branches."

For present purposes, we look to the Eastern Catholic Churches to consider a particular facet of ". . . the tradition that has been handed down from the Apostles through the Fathers that forms part of the divinely revealed and undivided heritage of the universal Church." A heritage to which the Second Vatican Council accorded ". . . the high regard which is its due and rightful praise."

A discussion of the unique history of each of the more than 20 distinct churches included among the Eastern Catholic Churches is beyond the scope of this work. Each Church traces its origin back to one of the patriarchiates which arose in the early centuries of the Christian era: Alexandria, Antioch, Constantinople or Jerusalem. Over time, the religious and political tensions which arose between the Church of Rome in the West and the Churches in the East precipitated the separation in 1054 which to the present day has not been completely healed. The Eastern Catholic Churches listed below represent only a portion of all Eastern Christians, the majority of whom generally are referred to as Orthodox Christians and are not yet in full communion with the Catholic Church.

An insight into the diverse history, traditions and abundant ecclesiastical institutions of the Eastern Catholic Churches may be gained by considering the residential episcopal sees of the heads of the individual Churches: Bherke, Lebanon; Baghgdad, Iraq; Ernakulum, India; Cairo, Egypt; Addis Ababa, Ethiopia; Trivandrum, Kerala State, India; Damascus, Syria; Lviv, Ukraine; Blaj, Romania; Athens, Greece; Zagreb, Croatia; Sofia, Bulgaria; Presov, Slovakia; and Nyireghaza, Hungary.

The names of individual Eastern Catholic Churches, together with the best available data on the total number of faithful and the number of faithful in the United States and Canada, are provided on the following page. [67]

159

Eastern Catholic Churches		
Churches	**Number of Faithful**	
	Total	**United States**
Maronite	3,222,000	55,000
Italo-Albanian	64,000	
Chaldean	304,000	65,000
Syro-Malaba	3,886,000	
Armenian	344,000	
Coptic	197,000	
Ethiopian	203,000	
Syrian	129,000	
Syro-Malankara	327,000	
Melkite	1,190,000	28,000
Ukrainian	5,182,000	121,000
Ruthenian	533,000	170,000
Romanian	1,119,000	
Greek*	49,000	
Bulgarian	15,000	
Slovak	222,00	
Hungarian	282,000	
Russians**	3,500	
Belarusans**	100,000	
Georgians**	unknown	
Albanians**	unknown	
		Canada
Melkite		43,000
Ukrainian		174,000
Slovak		20,000

*Greek Catholics in former Yugoslavia;

**Communities with no hierarchies.

The Second Vatican Council confirmed that the liturgical rites, ecclesiastical traditions and practices of the Eastern Catholic Churches by virtue of their venerable antiquity manifest the tradition that has been handed down from the Apostles through the Fathers. Further, the Council firmly asserted that the established standards of the Eastern Churches form part of the divinely revealed and undivided heritage of the universal Church. One such tradition and standard which the Eastern Churches, individually and jointly, have upheld and passed down without interruption from ancient times is the standard of optional celibacy for clerics prior to priestly ordination.

3. CANON LAW

"Teacher, which commandment in the law is the greatest?" He said to him, "You shall love the Lord, your God, with all your heart, with all your soul, and with all your mind. This is the greatest and first commandment. The second is like it: You shall love your neighbor as yourself. The whole law and the prophets depend on these two commandments." (Mt 22:36-40)

A discussion of canon law which is not founded upon these words of Jesus is a house built upon sand. The first criterion for judging each law of the church is: Do the purpose and means of implementing the law promote the love of God and the love of neighbor?

Unlike scripture, canon law lays no claim to divine inspiration. Canon law emerged piecemeal, at first in the form of the decrees of individual bishops and later in the canons enacted by councils of bishops. An early example was the regional Council of Elvira (c. 305) (see pp. 21-24) which issued the first known canon regarding priestly celibacy. In the course of succeeding centuries, partial collections of canons appeared in Italy, Africa, Germany and France and in the Churches of the East. However, it was left to the monk Gratian to assemble in 1140 the first definitive canonical collection for the Western Church. As is the case with all law, in the centuries following the "Decree of Gratian" an increasingly centralized administration of the Church continued to add to and revise the body of canon law.

To reflect the growth in the body of ecclesiastical law, a new compilation of canons was published in Paris in 1500 under the title of *Corpus Juris Canonici* (The Body of Canon Law). Another four centuries passed before Pope Pius X undertook the next major updating of canons which he promulgated on May 27, 1917 as the *Codex Juris Canonici* or Code of Canon Law. The 1917 code governed all aspects of the Western Church until Pope John Paul II promulgated the current Code of Canon Law on January 25, 1983, with an effective date of November 27, 1983.

The development of canon law for the Eastern Churches differed from the Church in the West. In the first centuries the Eastern Churches relied in large measure upon the New Testament, the writings of Apostolic Fathers and pseudo-apostolic writings. The Apostolic Canons (comprising some 85 canons), which were composed about 400 A.D., were also widely regarded. In 451 the Council of Chalcedon produced the *Corpus canonum orientale,* or Eastern Body of Canons. To these, other councils of the fifth and sixth centuries added their own canons. In 692 the Council of Trullo (see pp. 27-33) embraced previously enacted canons and added over 100 of its own, all of which it accepted as the official canonical code of the Eastern Churches. As with the West, canon law continued to evolve in the East and in 920 the *Nomocanon 14 titulorum* or Canon Law of 14 Titles was accepted as law for the Eastern Churches.

A thousand years later in 1929 Pope Pius XI established a commission of cardinals to codify canon law which was valid for all Eastern Catholic Churches. In 1935 the commission was elevated to the status of the Pontifical Commission for the Redaction of the *Codex Juris Canonici Orientalis* or the Code of Oriental Law.

Work on the code continued over the years but did not come to completion until seven years after the revised Code of Canon Law of the Latin Church was promulgated in 1983. In his remarks at the time of promulgation of the Code of Canons of the Eastern Churches on October 18, 1990, Pope John Paul II wrote:

> The Code of Canons of the Eastern Churches which now comes to light must be considered a new complement to the teachings proposed by the Second Vatican Council, and by which at last the canonical ordering of the entire Church is completed.[68]

This cursory historical review of the development of canon law in the West and in the East is interjected at this point for the following reasons:

1. To bring out the legitimate and equal nature of the canon law of the West and of the East, each of which has

arisen from the diverse historical, social, cultural and faith histories within the one undivided Church;

2. To emphasize the fact that canon law is in a continual process of evolution — as well it should be — in order to respond in a meaningful manner to the dynamics of a changing world and the changing needs of the People of God who are the Church.

The discussion that follows reviews canons which relate to sacred orders (primarily the priesthood) as they appear in the 1983 Code of Canon Law (CIC) for the Western Church and the 1990 Code of Canons of the Eastern Churches (CCEO). As the Editor's Note to the CCEO indicates: At times there is a literal correspondence among the canons; at other times there is substantial correspondence, at still other times there is only partial correspondence, and finally, at times there is no correspondence.[69]

PRIESTHOOD (CELIBATE AND/OR MARRIED)

LITERAL CORRESPONDENCE

An example of literal correspondence appears between:

CIC Can. 1009-§1. The orders are the episcopate, the priesthood and the diaconate.

CCEO Can. 325. In virtue of sacred ordination clerics are distinguished as bishops, presbyters, and deacons.

Can. 1024 of the CIC and Can. 754 of the CCEO are another example of literal verbal correspondence. Both canons state: Only a baptized man can validly receive sacred ordination.

A third example of literal correspondence is the following:

CIC Can. 1087. Those who are in sacred orders invalidly attempt marriage;

CCEO Can. 804. Persons who are in holy orders invalidly attempt marriage

PARTIAL CORRESPONDENCE

An example of partial correspondence appears in the discussion of celibacy shown below in the CIC Can. 277 and the CCEO Can. 373:

Can. 277-§1. Clerics are obliged to observe perfect chastity and perpetual continence for the sake of the kingdom of heaven, and are therefore bound to celibacy. Celibacy is a special gift of God by which sacred ministers can more easily remain close to Christ with an undivided heart and can dedicate themselves more freely to the service of God and their neighbor.

Can. 373. Clerical celibacy chosen for the sake of the kingdom of heaven and suited to the priesthood is to be greatly esteemed everywhere, as supported by the tradition of the whole Church; likewise, the hallowed practice of married clerics in the primitive Church and in the tradition of the Eastern Churches throughout the ages is to be held in honor.

While the CCEO provides for the possibility of either celibacy or marriage, the requirement for chastity is strongly emphasized as follows:

Can. 374. Clerics, celibate or married, are to excel in the virtue of chastity; it is for the particular law to establish suitable means of pursuing this end.

Both the CIC and CCEO are in agreement that clerical celibacy for the sake of the kingdom of heaven is to be highly regarded. The canons differ in that the CIC establishes an absolute link between the clerical state and celibacy, while the CCEO accepts both celibacy and marriage as consistent with the clerical state. Further, the CIC asserts that celibacy fosters greater service to God and others with an undivided heart, while the CCEO cites both the practice of the primitive church and the tradition of Eastern Churches in support of the rule of optional celibacy.

However, the CCEO in Can.758-§3 provides additional guidance on the subject of marriage and sacred orders. The canon states:

The particular law of each Church *sui juris* or special norms established by the Apostolic See are to be followed in admitting married men to sacred orders.

A particular example of "special norms established by the Apostolic See" is found in the history of married priests in North and South America and Australia.

In the 1870's, significant numbers of Eastern Catholics immigrated to the United States. Ignorance among Catholics of the Western Church regarding the practices of the Eastern Catholics, including married priests, led to conflicts with the American hierarchy. At the urging of certain members of the American hierarchy, the Holy See in 1905 issued the first of several proclamations, *Ea Semper*, which prohibited married clergy of the Eastern Churches from being sent to North America and restricted the ordination of married men in America.

The earlier prohibition was repeated several times, including two separate times in 1929. The Sacred Congregation for the Oriental Churches on March 1, 1929, issued the *Moto Proprio Cum Data Fuerit*, which was renewed November 30, 1940, and again November 23, 1950. Article 12 stated:

. . . as has already several times been decreed, priests of the Greek-Ruthenian Rite who wish to go to the United States of North America and stay there, must be celibates.[70]

On December 23, 1929, the Office of the Sacred Congregation for the Oriental Churches issued additional directives in the decree *Qua Sollerti* [71]which had legal force from April 1, 1930. The opening words identify the document as a:

DECREE ON MEMBERS OF THE ORIENTAL CLERGY, SECULAR OR REGULAR, WHO EMIGRATE FROM ORIENTAL TERRITORIES OR DIOCESES TO NORTH, CENTRAL OR SOUTH AMERICA, OR TO AUSTRALIA, WITH THE PURPOSE OF GIVING SPIRITUAL MINISTRATIONS TO THE FAITHFUL OF THEIR OWN RITE.

The decree states, in part:

6. Secular priests who are married will not be permitted to exercise the sacred ministry in the above countries, but only those who are celibates or widowers. For just reasons, however, the Sacred Congregation may exclude widowers from those dioceses and places in which or in the vicinity of which their children might perchance reside or otherwise be found.

Apparently, the Holy See was concerned not only that the presence of married clergy might confuse or scandalize the general Catholic population, but that the presence of the children of widowers who might contact their fathers also provided cause for concern.

The 1990 Code of Canons of the Eastern Churches does not include the restrictions which appeared in *Cum Data*

Fuerit or in *Qua Sollerti*. As a general rule, therefore, the restriction on married clergy which appeared in the earlier documents may be viewed as having been supplanted by the later canons. The requirement for candidates for sacred ordination to be ordained licitly which appear in Canon 758 does not preclude the ordination of married men. However, the Norms of Particular Law of the Byzantine Metropolitan Church *Sui Juris* of Pittsburgh (i.e., the Ruthenian Catholic Church)[72] which became effective as of October 1, 1999, require that approval must be obtained from the Holy See for each individual case in which a married man is proposed for ordination to the priesthood. The section of the norms which is cited below falls under CCEO Can. 758-§3 which states:

The particular law of each Church *sui juris* or special norms established by the Apostolic See are to be followed in admitting married men to sacred orders.

The Norms of Particular Law add:

§1. Married men, after completion of the formation prescribed by law, can be admitted to the order of deacon.

§2. Concerning the admission of married men to the order of the presbyterate, the special norms issued by the Apostolic See are to be observed, unless dispensations are granted by the same See in individual cases.

According to a reliable source, at the present time there are a scattering of about 8 to 10 married priests among the Melkite and Ukranian Catholic Churches in the United States. The Ruthenian Catholic Church presently has no married priests.

The United States National Conference of Catholic Bishops (NCCB) has not taken action to request that the Holy See permit married priests of the Eastern Churches to minister in the United States (an action which could effectively remove any ambiguity concerning the continued force of restrictions imposed by *Cum Data Fuerit*). However, the canonical commission of the NCCB is reported to have been in contact with the Holy See on the subject.

Meanwhile, on May 28, 1998, the Australian Conference of Catholic Bishops passed the following motion:

> The Australian Catholic Bishops Conference welcomes the development of the Ukranian, Maronite, and Melkite Eparchies in Australia. The Conference expresses its respect for the clergy, including the married clergy, working in the Eparchies and the other Eastern Catholic Churches. The Conference further affirms that it has no objection to the Eparchs ordaining married men to the diaconate and priesthood in Australia.[73]

A few married priests are ministering to the faithful of Eastern Churches in Australia.

Moving from the subject of who may be ordained to the opposite subject of who may not be ordained, it is found that on the subject of impediments to sacred orders the

171

provisions of the CCEO and the CIC in large measure are identical, with two notable distinctions.

The CCEO lists in Can. 762 eight categories of persons who are impeded from receiving sacred orders. The CIC in Can. 1040 distinguishes two types of impediments to orders: simple or perpetual. The latter is also called an irregularity. Can. 1041 lists as irregularities the first six impediments listed in the CCEO. Included are such matters as insanity, apostasy, heresy, schism, wilful homicide, procuring an abortion, self-mutilation, attempted suicide. Can. 1042 of the CIC lists as simple impediments the remaining two types of impediments given in CCEO Can. 762, and adds one additional simple impediment:

Can. 1042. The following are simply impeded from receiving orders:

1° a man who has a wife, unless he is lawfully destined for the permanent diaconate.

No comparable provision is found in the CCEO since marriage is not an impediment to the priesthood in the Eastern Churches.

Can. 1042, 1° of the CIC is the legal basis upon which the law of celibacy in the Western Church rests. Dispensations from this simple impediment are reserved to the Apostolic See (Can.1047, §2,1°). The Pastoral Provisions discussed in Chapter 3 rely upon such dispensations as the basis to permit married former sacred ministers of other

Christian communions to be ordained as Catholic priests.

The differing orientations of CIC and CCEO regarding celibacy and marriage appear also in the canons which consider the material needs of clerics.

The CIC states:

Can. 281-§1. Since clerics dedicate themselves to the ecclesiastical ministry, they deserve the remuneration that befits their condition, taking into account both the nature of their office and the conditions of time and place. It is to be such that it provides for the necessities of their life and for the just remuneration of those whose service they need.

§2. Suitable provision is likewise to be made for such social welfare as they may need in infirmity, sickness or old age.

The CCEO discusses the same subject in several canons as follows:

Can. 192-§5. The eparchial bishop is to see to it that the families of his clerics, if they are married, be provided with adequate support, appropriate protection and social security in addition to health insurance according to the norm of law.

Can. 278-§3. The protopresbyter is to take care that the pastors and their families, if they are married, whom he knows to be seriously ill, do not lack spiritual and material assistance and that the funerals of those who have died are celebrated with dignity. He is also to provide that when they are sick or have died the books, documents, sacred furnishings and other things which pertain to the Church are not lost or removed.

Can. 390-§1 Clerics have the right to a suitable sustenance and to receive a just remuneration for carrying out the office or function committed to them; in the case of married clerics, the sustenance of their families, unless this has been otherwise sufficiently provided, is to be taken into account.

§2. They also have the right that there be provided for themselves as well as for their families, if they are married, suitable pension funds, social security as well as health benefits. So that this right can be effectively put into practice clerics are bound by an obligation on their part to contribute to the fund spoken of in can. 1021-§2 according to the norm of the particular law.

Can. 1410. The imposition of penalties on a cleric must preserve for him what is necessary for his decent support, unless it is a case of deposition, in which event the hierarch is to see to it that the deposed who is truly in need because of the punishment is provided for in the best way possible, taking into account always his vested right to insurance and social security as well as health insurance for him and his family, if he is married.

PERMANENT DEACONS

The Second Vatican Council stated that "it will be possible in the future to restore the diaconate as a proper and permanent rank of the hierarchy . . . (and confer it) even upon married men, provided they be of more mature age, and also on suitable young men for whom, however, the law of celibacy must remain in force"

With the Apostolic Letter *Sacrum diaconatus ordinem* of June 18, 1967,[74] Pope Paul VI implemented the recommendation of the Second Vatican Council by determining general norms governing the restoration of the permanent diaconate. In 1968 the Holy See granted the request of the United States Bishops to reestablish the permanent diaconate in this country. The Apostolic Letter *Ad pascendum* of August 15, 1972[75] clarified the conditions for the admission and ordination of candidates to the diaconate and the essential elements of these norms subsequently passed into the Code of Canon Law promulgated by Pope John Paul II on January 25, 1983.

Particular sections of the CIC and CCEO which regulate the permanent diaconate are noted below.

CIC Can. 236. Those who aspire to the permanent diaconate are to be formed in the spiritual life and appropriately instructed in the fulfillment of the duties proper to that order, in accordance with the provisions made by the Episcopal Conference.

The CCEO does not utilize the term "permanent diaconate." Rather, it refers in Can. 354 to "deacons not destined for the priesthood."

In both the West and the East a man becomes a cleric through the reception of diaconate and incardination into a particular Church.

CIC Can. 266-§1. By the reception of the diaconate a person becomes a cleric, and is incardinated in the particular Church or Personal Prelature for whose service he is ordained.

CCEO Can. 358. Through diaconal ordination a man is enrolled as a cleric in the eparchy for whose service he is ordained unless, according to the norm of the particular law of his own Church *sui juris*, he has already been enrolled in the same eparchy.

The CIC and CCEO address the formation of permanent deacons with different provisions, but similar goals.

CIC Can. 236. Those who aspire to the permanent diaconate are to be formed in the spiritual life and appropriately instructed in the fulfillment of the duties proper to that order, in accordance with the provisions made by the Episcopal Conference.

CCEO Can. 354. The formation of deacons not destined for the priesthood is to be appropriately adapted from the norms given above so that the curriculum of studies extends at least three years keeping in mind the traditions of their own Church *sui juris* concerning the service of the liturgy, the word and charity. (The "norms given above" refer to a series of canons listed under Title X, Article II - Formation for Ministry.)

The CIC and CCEO approach the subject of remuneration from different perspectives.

The CIC includes a specific canon which concerns the remuneration of permanent deacons; whereas, the CCEO provides a single norm for remuneration of clerics in general, whether deacon, priest or bishop.

CIC Can. 281-§3. Married deacons who dedicate themselves fulltime to the ecclesiastical ministry deserve remuneration sufficient to provide for themselves and their families. Those, however, who receive a remuneration by reason of a secular profession which they exercise or exercised, are to see to their own and to their families' need from that income.

CCEO Can. 390-§1. Clerics have the right to a suitable sustenance and to receive a just remuneration for carrying out the office or function committed to them; in the case of married clerics, the sustenance of their families, unless this has been otherwise sufficiently provided, is to be taken into account.

§2. They also have the right that there be provided for themselves as well as for their families, if they are married, suitable pension funds, social security as well as health benefits. So that this right can be effectively put into practice clerics are bound by an obligation on their part to contribute to the fund spoken of in can. 1021, §2 according to the norms of particular law. (Can. 1021, §2 provides for the creation of institutes under the vigilance of the local hierarch to provide for social security and health insurance where other provisions have not been arranged.)

Notable differences appear between the CIC and CCEO. The CIC provides that full-time married deacons deserve sufficient remuneration, while the CCEO provides for just remuneration. The CCEO includes for permanent deacons pensions, health insurance and social security, none of which is mentioned in the CIC. The CIC provides that married deacons who receive remuneration from a secular profession are to provide for the needs of their families from such income. No mention is made as to the adequacy of the remuneration. On the other hand, the CCEO clearly provides the right of married deacons to remuneration unless the needs of the deacons and their families are sufficiently provided for in another manner.

4. PRIESTHOOD TODAY

In June 2000 the National Conference of Catholic Bishops (NCCB) released summary information about a study which had been carried out for the Bishops' Committee on Priestly Life and Ministry by the Center for Applied Research in the Apostolate (CARA)based at Georgetown University. The title is: *The Study of the Impact of Fewer Priests on the Pastoral Ministry.*[76]

The three-part study which was carried out between the fall of 1998 and the spring of 2000:

1) reviewed statistical trends for the last hundred years as related to the total Catholic population, as well as the numbers of: dioceses and eparchies, parishes, priests, Catholics per parish, and Catholics per priest;

2) collected current demographic data on: all priests in the United States, the ethnic diversity of the Catholic population, geographic distribution of Catholics, the numbers of seminarians, permanent deacons and lay ecclesial ministers;

3) conducted focus groups with priests (18), deacons (3), and lay ministers (3) to consider the topic of parish ministry in a time of fewer priests; and

4) conducted a national telephone poll of 2,635 Catholics to elicit the views of ordinary Catholics about the decreasing number of priests in the United States.

In the Introduction to Supplementary Document "D" of the study which was made available to the Bishops at their

Spring General Meeting in Milwaukee, Wisconsin, on June 15 -17, 2000, and to others upon request, Bishop Richard Hanifen, Chairman, Bishops' Committee on Priestly Life and Ministry, noted:

> What is the purpose of this study? From the outset, we did not want to collect yet another book of data. Our hope all along has been simply to provide reliable data to enable a dialogue among us as brother bishops. We have resisted interpreting the data that we are about to present to you. We have, however, asked each of the eight chairmen to include in our resource book a reflection on the data from the point of view of his committee. These same committees have also raised questions in their reflections that we hope will assist to focus the ensuing dialogue. Today we will begin this dialogue. We believe it will continue for a while. It will need to, and it will need to be done carefully. We look for no action items at the end of today's dialogue. We do ask that as we go through the workshop you might make notes that you might later on develop into suggestions for action, or further study by various conference committees.[77]

Initially it should be clarified that, despite its title, the study is not, nor was it intended to be, an impact study. Rather, the report presents the results of a combination statistical survey and poll of opinions, actions and plans related to the topic of the study. The remarks of Bishop Hanifen make clear that the intent of the study was to provide reliable data for the purpose of enabling dialogue among the bishops and that the authors of the study resisted interpreting the data; that is, they did not assess the impact of the data.

Bishop Hanifen makes no mention of anyone, other than the bishops, being involved in dialogue on the data. Therefore, the observations which follow are an uninvited, but hopefully constructive, contribution to the dialogue mentioned by Bishop Hanifen.

First, it is regrettable that the Conference of Bishops has chosen to restrict general access to the entire study and has limited public information to the data contained in Supplementary Document "D". While the supplementary information is valuable, a truly informed and meaningful dialogue can take place only when all elements of the complete study (including: statement of purpose, investigative restraints, sample selection method, data collection instruments and methodology, identified strengths and weaknesses of outcomes) are made available.

Second, to be credible, dialogue on the subject of "The Impact of Fewer Priests on the Pastoral Ministry," must include appropriate provision for the voices of all affected parties, especially the laity, to be heard and respected. Hopefully, when the bishops consider action steps in response to the findings of the study, they will resolve to initiate dialogue in each diocese with the inclusion of broad-based lay involvement from each parish.

Third, the dialogue should be allowed freely to explore all forms of alternative responses to the issue which are not contradictory to revealed truth or defined Church dogma, including those which might involve exceptions to or waivers of existing Church discipline.

A. Statistical Data

The statistical data presented in the study fall into three broad categories:
1) data which are compared at 50 year intervals: 1900, 1950, 2000;
2) data compared over more limited periods: 1960-1999, 1970-2000;
3) most recent year data.

While all interested parties, Catholics and others, should have reasonable access to all of the data contained in the study, much of the data exceeds the interest of this book. Therefore, only select data are cited here and drawn together to form a foundation for material which appears in the final chapter of the book.

The first relevant data are that in the year 2000 there were 59,156,237 Catholics in 19,181 parishes in the United States. The study also notes that there are 192 dioceses and eparchies in the United States.[78] The number of Catholics represents a 107 percent increase since 1950 when Catholics numbered 28,634,878. The statistics for priests in the same 50 year period were quite different. In the year 2000 the study found that there were 46,709 priests in the United States, a figure which represented only a six percent increase over the number of priests in 1950.[79] The outline of the issue immediately begins to take shape with just these few data.

The growth in Catholic population in the last 50 years has dramatically outstripped the growth in the number of priests. Nor is there any sign of a change in the trend. The study notes that the Catholic population continues to increase at a steady rate;[80] while, for each of the last 30 years, the total number of diocesan priests has decreased from the number in the preceding year.[81] The decrease is explained by the fact that each year the total number of priests who have died or left the active priesthood has exceeded the total number of newly ordained.

Not counted in the "net loss" are the additional number of priests who retire each year. Among the 46,709 total priests in the United States, 9,524, or 20 percent, were retired.[82] The study reports that the average age found for diocesan priests was 57 years and the average age of religious priests was 63 years. Only 298 priests were found to be under 30 years old while 433 were over 90 years old.[83] The numbers of tomorrow's priests presently enrolled in seminaries do not offer reason to expect a dramatic improvement in the present situation. Theology-level seminary enrollment in 2000 was 3,474 students, down from 3,609 just ten years ago, and from a high of 6,602 in 1970.[84]

[Data from the 2001 Official Catholic Directory update the information contained in the CARA study. The Directory reports that Catholic population has risen to nearly 63.7 million. Additionally, the Directory confirms the continuing annual decline in the number of priests. The 30,655 diocesan priests reported represent 285 less than the prior year's figure; and the 15,386 religious order priests show a decrease of 79 in the same period. Overall, the Directory notes that the total number of priests in the United States declined by 325 between 2000 and 2001 reports. These data continue the annual downward trend line shown in the CARA study.]

The total number and ages of priests are important, but not exclusive, factors to consider in a study of impact on pastoral ministry. Another important consideration is the availability of the priests for pastoral ministry.

The study reports that in 2000 the ratio of Catholics per priest was 1,257: 1.[85] In considering this ratio it is important to give due weight to the accompanying note which says that: The number includes all Catholics and all priests in the United States: active, retired, diocesan and religious. Stated differently, that means that the ratio includes the 9,524 priests who are retired, as well as all other priests, regardless of the nature of their assignments. Mathematically the number is accurate, but it has no direct relation to the topic, namely, impact on pastoral ministry.

At least five elements are of basic importance to consider in a discussion of the impact of fewer priests on pastoral ministry:
1. Total number of Catholics
2. Total number of dioceses and eparchies
3. Total number of parishes
4. Total number of priests active in pastoral ministry
5. Distribution of Catholics, priests and parishes.

The total number of Catholics (59,156,237), dioceses and eparchies (192), and parishes (19, 181) have already been established. What then may be said of the total number of priests who are active in pastoral ministry? The study indicates that 27,015 priests (22,394 diocesan and 4,621 religious) were active in parish ministry in 2000.[86] Put in other terms, on average there were 2,190 Catholics per priest engaged in active pastoral ministry and 1.4 priests per parish in the United States.

Such data, at best, provide a general idea of the pastoral ministry situation. Certainly, the current numbers might appear better than a situation, for example, where the ratio was 5,000 Catholics per priest engaged in pastoral ministry. However, an assessment of impact can hardly begin without introducing the fifth element mentioned above—distribution. Statistical averages do not deal with questions of extremes of range in the density of Catholic population, the concentration — or paucity —of priests in some areas, the impact of geographic distances, the autonomy of individual dioceses and eparchies, and a host of other variables.

A few variables referenced in the study are the following:

1. Eighty-two percent of dioceses and eparchies report that they have fewer priests relative to their pastoral needs compared to a decade ago.[87]

2. Sixteen percent of priests active in parish or diocesan ministry are foreign born.[88]

3. Of the total 19,181 parishes about 73 percent (or 14,026 parishes), have a resident full-time pastor. The remaining 27 percent of parishes either: share a pastor with one or more other parishes (2,386 parishes), have no resident pastor (2,334 parishes), or are entrusted to someone other than a priest (437 parishes).[89]

Given that pastoral ministry in today's Church includes a wide range of others in the Christian community, in addition to priests, the study offers the following data as relevant to the subject under consideration:

1. Currently there are almost 13,000 deacons who serve in almost all dioceses and eparchies; over 2,500 men are in formation for the diaconate.[90]

2. There are about 30,000 paid professional pastoral associates, directors of religious education, music ministers, and other parish ministers. Another 12,000 serve in parish youth ministry; 30,000 Catholics are in degree-granting or certificate programs preparing for ministry; about 150,000 lay teachers work in Catholic schools; and another 5,000 lay ministers are employed at campus, hospital, prison and other ministry sites.[91]

B. Pastoral Strategies

In view of the present reality of a shortage of priests and the future expectation of an even more critical shortage in years to come, what strategies and plans did the study find have been, or are being, developed to provide in an adequate manner for the pastoral ministry of a steadily increasing number and diversity of the total Catholic population?

The pastoral strategies identified which are currently in use, or expected to be initiated in the future, include the following:

Among vocation strategies the study noted that four in five dioceses have a plan for priestly vocations; four in five dioceses help priests recruit vocations; and all dioceses report that renewed efforts to foster priestly vocations are essential. Further details were not included in Document "D".

In addition to the traditional pattern of having a pastor of a single parish, the parish strategies reported include the following as currently employed and/or expected to be utilized in the coming years: 1. Having one pastor administer multiple parishes; 2. Entrusting the pastoral care of the parish to someone other than a priest under the authority of can. 517.2; 3. Having several priests serve as a team to minister to one or more parishes under authority of can. 517.1; 4. Organizing the ministry of priests after retirement; 5. Closing parishes; 6. Sharing ministry staff among parishes; 7. Reducing the number of masses.

In the area of collaboration in ministry by deacons and other ecclesial ministers the study reports that today a majority of dioceses "somewhat" or "very much": 1. Have increased the assignment of deacons for sacramental or liturgical ministry; 2. Employ deacons or lay persons in parish management. An even larger majority of dioceses anticipate in the future assigning deacons or lay persons to assist in parish management. A similar pattern is reported for the use of lay ecclesial ministers in diocesan offices and institutions.

Can. 517 which is referenced above reads as follows:

§1. Where circumstances so require, the pastoral care of a parish, or of a number of parishes together, can be entrusted to several priests jointly, but with the stipulation that one of the priests is to be the moderator of the pastoral care to be exercised. The moderator is to direct the joint action and to be responsible to the Bishop.

§2. If, because of a shortage of priests, the diocesan Bishop has judged that a deacon, or some other person who is not a priest, or a community of priests, should be entrusted with a share in the exercise of the pastoral care of a parish, he is to appoint some priest who, with the powers and faculties of a parish priest, will direct the pastoral care.

At the time of the study, a total of 271 priests were members of a priest team under can. 517.1. The study data summary does not reveal how many parishes were served by these team members. Also, 437 parishes were reported to be entrusted to someone other than a priest under can. 517.2.[92] Data on the number of parishes closed or combined were not included in Document "D".

TOMORROW

Chapter 4

ONCE OVER LIGHTLY

Before considering prospects for the future in an era of continued disparity between the increasing shortage of priests and the rapid growth in the Catholic population, we pause to briefly review the past and present which has led us to this point

Scripture confirms that Jesus did not consider the marital status of His disciples when He called each of them to follow Him or when He raised them to the priesthood at the Last Supper. Whether Peter, Andrew, James, John or the other Apostles were, or were not, married was immaterial. The criterion of their vocation was not marital status, but total dedication to Jesus personally, to His teachings, and to His mission of redemption.

For the first three centuries of Christianity, the Church focus was upon survival in a hostile environment and upon spreading the Good News to all parts of the earth as Jesus had commanded. Priests freely exercised the option to marry or to remain celibate. The first recorded attempt to impose a requirement of priestly celibacy in the Church of the West did not appear until the Council of Elvira early in the fourth century.

For the next eight centuries, an increasingly centralized hierarchy repeatedly sought to impose clergy celibacy with mixed results. It remained for Lateran Council II in the twelfth century finally to decree that all marital unions of priests were not true marriages — even those marriages that had been accepted as valid, albeit illicit, prior to the decree of the council. In effect, the council's canon disregarded the teaching of Jesus that what God had joined together no man — or council — should separate. Thereafter, the Council of Trent and subsequent canon law reaffirmed the requirement of perpetual celibacy for priests of the Western Church.

Nonetheless, as discussed in Chapter 3, p. 57, Pope Paul VI in 1967 opened the door to the limited possibility of married Catholic priests in the West. In 1980 Pope John Paul II granted approval to the Bishops of the United States, and in subsequent years to Conferences of Bishops in Canada, and England and Wales, to ordain to the priesthood married former sacred ministers of the Episcopalian/Anglican tradition who entered into full communion with the Catholic Church.

In addition, individual bishops have sought and obtained rescripts to ordain married former ministers of other Christian denominations.

Meanwhile, the tradition of optional celibacy has continued to be observed without interruption in Eastern Catholic Churches. The seventh century Council of Trullo reaffirmed absolutely the ancient tradition which permitted a man to marry before entering the clergy. All Eastern Catholic Churches continue to observe this norm which is included in the Code of Canons of the Eastern Churches that was approved by Pope John Paul II in 1990.

We come next to a looming crisis which already is having an impact and within a decade will drastically affect the entire Church and the spiritual lives of many, or possibly most, Catholics in the United States. Confronted openly and with a willingness to take action, the crisis in large measure possibly may be greatly mitigated, if not eliminated.

The Catholic population of the United States in the year 2000 was 59,156,237 and was steadily increasing in both total number and diversity. To respond to the needs of the faithful, 19,181 parishes existed in 192 dioceses and eparchies across the country. The average parish included 3,086 Catholics, while some fast-growing parishes in at least one diocese were expected soon to include up to 18,000 households.[93] At the other end, parishes with only a few hundred parishioners also could be found.

To meet the spiritual needs of the nearly 60 million Catholics, there was a total of 46,709 diocesan and religious priests, of whom 9,541, or one in five, were retired. Of the remaining 37,168 priests in active ministry, only 27,015 were engaged in parish ministry, for an average of 1.4 priests per parish.[94] The real world, of course, does not consist of average parishes, each with 3,086 parishioners, and each ministered to by 1.4 priests. Independent dioceses and eparchies each cover greater or smaller territories, include highly urban centers and /or vast rural areas, have greater or lesser concentrations of Catholics, and have notable variances in the numbers of priests engaged in the active ministry.

Adding a further dimension to the picture is the reality that roughly half of all priests are 60 years of age or older, with the common retirement age being about 70. The aging of the priest population would be of less significance were it not for another reality, namely, the replacement number of future priests in training at seminaries across the country falls far short of the number needed simply to maintain the current level of priest population, let alone provide an increased supply of priests that would be sufficient to meet the ministerial needs of a rapidly growing number of Catholics in future years. In 2000 the theology level seminarian enrollment was 3,474, a decrease of 135 since 1990 and of 3,128 since 1970.[95]

A decline in the total number of priests has been evident since the late 1960's when the number of priests lost to death and departures each year began to exceed the number of newly ordained. The net loss in the total number of priests for 1999 alone was about 400.[96] The annual net loss in total priests noted for each of the last 30 years may be expected to continue in the future.

Using three models (optimistic, moderate and pessimistic) to project the size of the diocesan priest population by the year 2015, Young[97] offers the following projections:

optimistic	21,863 priests
moderate	19,050 priests
pessimistic	13,568 priests

He clarifies his projections in these words:
The projections focus on the population of active priests, meaning the total number of incardinated diocesan priests with an official work assignment either inside or outside the diocese. Priests on study leave, on loan outside the diocese, or on duty as military chaplains, and so on, are included in the estimates and projections. Priests who have been on sick leave or awaiting assignment for at least 12 months, as well as retired priests, are not included.

Based on the highly accurate projection models reported by Young and his associate, Schoenherr, in their

1993 book, *Full pews and empty altars,* Young states that, under the moderate conditions which have marked the recent past and are reasonable to assume for the future, the decline in priest population by 2015 will reach 46 percent — creating a loss of more than 16,000 priests since 1966. Since Young's estimate refers solely to diocesan priests, the decrease among religious priests would be in addition to his figure.

Given that there is no evidence of a dramatic reversal in the declining number of priests in the immediate future, some point with optimism to the growing number of permanent deacons and ecclesial lay ministers in the Church. In 1999 there were 12,862 permanent deacons in the United States serving in almost all parts of the country. Ninety-one percent of deacons were married men. Four percent were widowed, three percent divorced and three percent were single (never married). An additional 2,582 candidates for the diaconate were in formation programs.[98]

Because of the shortage of priests, deacons in 1999 had full-time pastoral care of 81 parishes, and were part-time administrators of parishes in 24 dioceses.[99] All would acknowledge the great service which the permanent diaconate has provided since it was reestablished by the Second Vatican Council and will continue to offer to the church in the United States and in countries around the world. However, few, if any, would argue that greater numbers of permanent deacons will compensate fully for the decline in the numbers of priests engaged in parish ministry.

The CARA study elicited from dioceses the methods presently in place or anticipated to be implemented to respond to the shortage of priests. The responses of dioceses included: having a vocation plan and helping priests recruit vocations; assigning one pastor to administer multiple parishes; entrusting the pastoral care of parishes to someone other than a priest; organizing the ministry of priests after retirement; closing parishes; sharing ministry staff; reducing the number of masses; increasing the sacramental or liturgical ministry of deacons; employing deacons or lay persons in parish management; increasing the number of lay ecclesial ministers in parishes, diocesan offices or institutions.[100]

The varied list of pastoral strategies offered by the dioceses have about them one common element which at first might not be evident. That common element is: all responses proceed from an assumption that the parameters of the issue are fixed. The parameters being an understanding that any modification in the disciplinary rule of a celibate clergy required by canon 1042 must not even be considered among the possible pastoral strategies to meet the needs of a rapidly growing Catholic population in the face of sharply reduced numbers of celibate priests. All proposed solutions must be based upon the sole paradigm of a celibate clergy. In business terms, this would represent a classic example of "thinking in the box." The existing rules for doing something may never be changed.

At this point it is appropriate to clarify three points:

1. The CARA study by intent did not include any references to ordination issues, since it was recognized that the data on that subject have already been well documented. Over several decades the laity has strongly supported the ordination of married men (as well as permitting the return to active ministry of married priests and the ordination to the priesthood of women). Most recently, in three separate surveys conducted in 1987, 1993 and 1999 American Catholics responded with strong affirmation to the question of whether it would be a good thing if married men were allowed to be ordained. Seventy-one percent of the respondents to the 1999 survey favored allowing married men to be ordained.[101]

2. The history and present practice of the Eastern Catholic Churches provide indisputable witness to the scriptural, dogmatic, canonical and pastoral acceptability of a priesthood which includes both celibate and married priests.

3. As discussed on page 100, there already exists in the Latin Church a group of married priests who are active in 48 dioceses across the United States and in several other countries. Therefore, there is precedent to include in a study about the impact of a shortage of priests on pastoral ministry consideration of the appropriateness of expanding the number of married priests already ministering in the Church in favor of the pastoral needs of the faithful.

CANON LAW REPORT

The Canon Law Society of America (CLSA) has had a long-standing interest in the topic of a married priesthood. As early as 1970, CLSA resolved to study the canonical institutions of the clerical state, celibacy and ministry, and the possibility of new canonical forms allowing their separation or their different combination.[102]

In 1971 the Society sponsored a symposium on "the Future Discipline of Priestly Celibacy." [103] Several years after the1980 approval of the Pastoral Provision, CLSA in 1987 commissioned a modest study of the practice of ordaining married men.[104] Richard A. Hill, S.J., author of the study, presented his findings in a seminar at the 1989 convention.[105] Key elements of Hill's report are found in this book at page 89. Again in 1991 CLSA resolved to commission a study of the canonical implications related to the ordination of married men to the priesthood in the United States.[106] An initial report was presented to CLSA in 1994 which, in turn, led to a determination to undertake a more complete investigation of the topic and the creation of a new *Ad Hoc* Committee.

On June 1, 1996, the *Ad Hoc* Committee of James A. Coriden and James H. Provost submitted to CLSA their report titled: *Canonical Implications Related to the Ordination of Married Men to the Priesthood in the United*

States of America.[107] The discussion which follows relies extensively upon the report content and research.

The Introduction to the report notes immediately that celibacy is "a special gift of God" (CIC c. 277, §1) that is required for clerics in the Latin Church and held in high esteem in the Eastern Churches (CCEO c. 373). The report then provides several approved exceptions to the general rule of celibacy for:

1. Married clerics in the Eastern Catholic Churches (CCEO c. 383),

2. Married deacons in the Latin Church (CIC c. 1042, 1°)

3. Married former sacred ministers of some other Christian church or ecclesial community, each of whom requires a dispensation from the Holy See from the simple impediment to orders ("a man who has a wife" CIC cc 1042, 1°, 1047, §2, 3).

The report authors stress that the canonical considerations discussed in their report "address the specific issues raised when married men are considered for ordination or have been ordained." They add that:

> The issues addressed in this report apply to the present situations described above; they would also apply to any other situation in which the

competent ecclesiastical authorities were to determine to permit the ordination of married men to the priesthood. Such a determination need not be for the entire Latin Church; in parallel with the provisions of the Eastern code (CCEO c. 758, §3), particular legislation could be authorized by the Apostolic See for individual episcopal conferences.[108]

The first major division of the report is: Entrance into Sacred Ministry, with subsections which discuss discernment of vocation, formation for ministry, irregularities and impediments.

The report makes clear in discussing Discernment of Vocation that the entire Christian community has the responsibility to foster vocations to sacred ministry; however, the appropriate bishop alone is responsible, with the assistance and advice of his appointees, to discern the vocation of a candidate for sacred orders. For candidates seeking ordination under the pastoral provision, additional authorities are involved, as is explained in Chapter 3.

Following present practice, the written consent of his wife must be obtained by a married candidate for sacred orders as: 1. A permanent deacon (CIC C. 1050, 3), 2. A priest ordained under the pastoral provision (Canadian "Procedures" n. 3,7), or 3. A priest in an Eastern Catholic Church (CCEO c. 769 (§1, 2°). The report states: "The canonical implications seem to be that for married men who petition for ordination, the consent of their wives is necessary." [109]

It is the opinion of the report authors that, while the consent of their wives is required of married men, "it may not be necessary to subject the discernment of their vocation to other authorities beyond the diocesan bishop provided the candidates have never ministered in another church or ecclesial community."[110] For example, in the case of a married Catholic born and raised in the faith, a sponsoring bishop might submit a request for dispensation directly to the Holy See without the need to proceed through an intermediary, such as an Ecclesiastical Delegate.

In discussing Formation for Ministry, the report authors address an issue which for many might appear to be a major stumbling block to the ordination of married men. Those who oppose ordaining married men might ask, "How possibly could a married man leave his family for four or more years of study and training at a seminary without serious harm to the family?" How indeed? The response of the report is that married priest candidates do not have to go away to a seminary. They point out that the Latin Church already takes advantage of canon 235 § 2, which provides for those legitimately living outside a seminary, for married men preparing for the permanent deaconate and for clergy of other churches received into full communion in the Catholic Church who petition for ordination to the priesthood.

In light of these precedents, it appears an accepted practice in the Latin Church that more mature men who are preparing for ordination, and who are married, need not be required to move to a seminary, but may remain living with their families and prepare for ordination using an alternative method. This does not exempt them, however, from the requirement to obtain the appropriately adapted philosophical and theological formation required before a candidate may be ordained. [111]

On the subject of Irregularities and Impediments the report reiterates the provisions of the CIC: marriage constitutes a simple impediment to orders except for those destined for the permanent diaconate (c. 1042, 1°); dispensation from this impediment is reserved to the Apostolic See (c. 1047, §2, 3°).

In cases of candidates seeking to be ordained under the pastoral provision in effect for particular countries: the United States, Canada, England and Wales, applications are submitted to the Congregation for the Doctrine of the Faith through the established Ecclesiastical Delegate system in each country. In countries which do not have a pastoral provision, petitions on behalf of non-Catholic clergy who seek Catholic ordination would be submitted to the Congregation for the Doctrine of the Faith directly by the sponsoring bishop.

The report takes note of the present restriction imposed by the Congregation for the Doctrine of the Faith upon married priests ordained under the Pastoral Provision, namely that these priests are not to be assigned to the "ordinary care of souls" and may not be appointed as pastors of parishes, except in the case of Anglican-use parishes. By exception, ordinaries may permit married priests to carry out the full range of priestly duties but, in no case, may married priests have all the responsibilities which fall to those who hold the office of parish priest.

The Congregation for the Doctrine of the Faith has chosen not to identify whether this restriction is imposed because of the prior service of these priests as sacred ministers in another church, or because of their married state, or because of some other reason. A clarification of the reason may arise indirectly the first time that an ordinary submits a married candidate for ordination who was born, raised and married in the Catholic Church. Although, even then, a clear answer may not be forthcoming. Such a case would not be submitted to the Congregation for the Doctrine of the Faith since it would not involve potential heresy or schism. In the case of a married Catholic man who has never been a sacred minister in another Christian tradition, the sponsoring ordinary may submit the application for a dispensation directly to the Congregation for Divine Worship and the Discipline of the Sacraments, which is competent to grant dispensations for impediments or irregularities which do not involve heresy or schism.[112]

As a condition for ordination, a candidate must be judged by the ordinary as useful for the Church (can. 1025, §2). There are no specific canonical norms given to guide the ordinary in this area, but it may be expected that an ordinary who is faced with an extreme shortage of priests, the possible or actual closing of parishes, and the availability of a well-qualified, dedicated married man might well consider that he would be useful to the Church. Since the reason for seeking the dispensation would be the shortage of priests to serve as pastors, the current ruling of the Congregation for the Doctrine of the Faith which restricts married priests from serving as pastors would have no relevance.

Concerning the applicability of these circumstances to the subject of the report, Coriden and Provost note:

> The canonical implication from this is that no special structure or procedures need be employed in processing petitions for ordination of married men who have not served as clergy in some other church or ecclesial community. The usual procedures for seeking a dispensation would be employed in approaching the Congregation for Divine Worship and the Discipline of the Sacraments for a dispensation from the impediment of canon 1042, 1. Once the dispensation has been obtained, the diocesan bishop can dispense from the promise of celibacy which is

to be made before the ordination of deacons who intend to seek eventual ordination to the presbyterate. (c. 1037).[113]

Under the heading of Obligations and Rights of Clergy several additional areas which have canonical implications are included in the report. Two of the areas are discussed below: Continence and Celibacy, Financial Support and Benefits.

On the subject of Continence and Celibacy the report states in part:

> In the Latin Church, "clergy are obliged to observe perfect and perpetual continence for the sake of the kingdom of heaven" (c. 277, §1).

> The dispensation from the impediment of canon 1042, 1° which permits a married man to be ordained to the priesthood does not explicitly include with it a dispensation from the obligations of canon 277, §1. Neither is there an explicit exception in the law for married men ordained to the diaconate. However, in virtue of canon 4, the acquired rights of married persons are not abrogated by the 1983 code and the marital rights of married clergy (c. 1135) override the

restrictions in canon 277, §1. However, as the
Apostolic See has emphasized regarding the
dispensation, the obligation of celibacy
remains in the event that the priest's wife dies;
he may not remarry.[114]

Financial Support and Benefits are discussed separately
in the report but combined here as being closely related.

Individual clerics who dedicate themselves to the
ecclesiastical ministry have a right to "remuneration which is
consistent with their condition."(c. 281, §1) The report
authors affirm that the "condition" of being married should
be considered in determining the level of financial support.
Since the Church clearly supports the right of lay ministers
(c. 231, §2) and permanent deacons (c. 281, §3) to receive a
decent remuneration for themselves and their families, the
report authors conclude the canonical implication that
married priests have a right to a family wage.[115]

Similarly, the authors conclude that the requirement
in CIC c. 281, §2 which prescribes that provision be made
for a priest's needs from "illness, incapacity, or old age"
would extend, as well, to the family of a married priest. This
conclusion is consistent with the content of the CCEO which
states that clergy, "have the right that there be provided for
themselves as well as for their families, if they are married,
suitable pension funds, social security as well as health
benefits" (CCEO c. 390, §2). [116]

SIGNS of the TIME

He also said to the crowds, "When you see a cloud rising in the west you say immediately that it is going to rain — and so it does; and when you notice that the wind is blowing from the south you say that it is going to be hot — and so it is. You hypocrites! You know how to interpret the appearance of the earth and sky; why do you not know how to interpret the present time?" (Lk 12: 54-56)

As we reflect on these sharp words of rebuke which Jesus addressed to the crowds in Luke 12 and to the Pharisees and Sadducees in Matthew 16, we may identify with his reaction to the hardness of heart and closed minds of the people of his time. How possibly could they have failed to see in Him the Promised Messiah, the fulfillment of the law and the prophets? How, despite the boundless love and compassion which he had shown to the least among them, despite the wisdom of his teachings which confounded their greatest scholars, despite the countless miracles which marked his passing throughout all of Judea, Galilee and even Samaria?

Yet, before we too quickly point to the speck in our brother's eye, let us consider the possible beam in our own.

The first words of Jesus are words of praise, not of rebuke. He acknowledges and respects the ability of his listeners to correctly use their God-given sensory perception. Then drawing upon their memory of past similar phenomena, they apply their intellectual ability to forecast the likelihood of a future event. "You say immediately that it is going to rain — and so it does." They know how to interpret the appearance of the earth and sky, and apply that interpretation in matters of daily life: to plant a crop today in the hope of rain tomorrow, or to complete a task quickly to avoid the approaching heat.

Why then does Jesus rebuke them? Because, he says, they do not know how to interpret the present time. "You, hypocrites!" he scolds them. Is his accusation fair? He has just said that they do not know how to interpret the present time. Are they liable for what they do not know? Is the child at fault because he does not know how to drive? Is the deaf man to be blamed because he does not answer our call? The difference, of course, and the foundation of Jesus' rebuke, is: They should have known how to interpret the present time. They should have known that he came as the Messiah. They had the witness of His life among them, His teachings, His example of unconditional love. They had the scriptural testimony of Moses and the prophets that they failed to heed because of their own bias and prejudiced notion that the Messiah must come as a worldly leader who would free them from Roman rule and restore the glory of Israel.

The audience to whom Jesus spoke does not stand alone. Throughout history, examples abound of individuals, leaders, nations, and even the Church, not knowing how to interpret the present time.

If the weatherman predicts a hurricane along the Florida coast, we hasten to board up our homes and withdraw to higher ground. If the Center for Disease Control announces an early outbreak of flu, we rush to get our shots. If the flow of foreign gas is shut off or seriously threatened, we consider twice the wisdom of purchasing a new mobile home. We carefully gather and study all possible information to help plan almost all important — and some not so important — aspects of our lives: choice of a career, location of a new home, a change of job, saving for retirement, the model of a new car.

Beyond our personal lives, if our responsibilities involve directing a major corporation or institution where our decisions impact the lives of significant numbers of other people, we gather and analyze all available data, engage experts, utilize advanced scientific technology, develop and test alternative models, initiate field tests, assess and evaluate outcomes, and, hopefully, determine a future course confident that we have done all that is possible "to interpret the present time."

Interesting, perhaps, but of what relevance, if any, you might ask, is this lengthy discussion of the passage in Chapter 12 of Luke's gospel to the subject of this book?

You ask a fair question. However, before responding, permit me yet one more apparent digression, a return to the final dialogue between Jesus and Peter which appears in the prologue.

> When they had finished breakfast, Jesus said to Simon Peter, "Simon, son of John, do you love me more than these?" He said to him, "Yes, Lord, you know that I love you." He said to him, "Feed my lambs." He then said to him a second time, "Simon, son of John, do you love me?" He said to him, "Yes, Lord, you know that I love you." He said to him, "Tend my sheep." He said to him the third time, "Simon, son of John, do you love me?" Peter was distressed that he had said to him a third time, "Do you love me?" And he said to him, "Lord, you know everything; you know that I love you." Jesus said to him, "Feed my sheep." (Jn 21:15-17)

Poor Peter! He was a fisherman who did not know much about sheep and shepherds, except that he saw them often grazing on the hillside outside of town. Now, as witness of his love, Jesus instructs him, not once, but three times:

"Feed my lambs." "Tend my sheep." "Feed my sheep."

This was not the first time that Jesus identified Himself as a shepherd and referred to his followers as sheep. Peter recalled the instance when Jesus, speaking to the crowd, identified Himself as the shepherd who entered the sheepfold through the open gate. He said, "The sheep hear his voice, as he calls his own sheep by name and leads them out. When he has driven out all his own, he walks ahead of them, and the sheep follow him, because they recognize his voice . . . I am the good shepherd and I know mine and mine know me, just as the Father knows me and I know the Father; and I will lay down my life for the sheep. I have other sheep that do not belong to this fold. These also I must lead, and they will hear my voice, and there will be one flock, one shepherd" (Jn 10:11, 14-16).

Then there was the time that Jesus told the parable of the lost sheep. As the tax collectors and sinners drew near to listen to Jesus, the Pharisees and the Scribes began to complain. Jesus asked them: "What man among you having a hundred sheep and losing one of them would not leave the ninety-nine in the desert and go after the one until he finds it? And when he does find it, he sets it on his shoulders with great joy and, upon his arrival home, he calls together his friends and neighbors and says to them, 'Rejoice with me because I have found my lost sheep.' I tell you, in just the same way there will be more joy in heaven over one sinner who repents than over ninety-nine righteous people who have no need of repentance." (Lk 15:4-7)

Even before Jesus called him, whenever Peter was troubled, he found comfort in the song of David:

The Lord is my shepherd, I shall not want.
In verdant pastures he gives me repose;
Beside restful waters he leads me, he refreshes
my soul.
He guides me in right paths for his name's
sake.
Even though I walk in the dark valley, I fear
no evil; for you are at my side.
With your rod and your staff that give me
courage.
You spread the table before me in the sight of
my foes;
You anoint my head with oil; my cup
overflows.
Only goodness and kindness follow me all the
days of my life.
And I shall dwell in the house of the Lord for
years to come. (Ps. 23)

Peter knew that Jesus, his Lord, was the shepherd of whom David sang. Jesus, the tender, loving shepherd, who, in truth, gave His life for his sheep, now in three brief words appointed him, a stumbling, unlearned man, as shepherd of His flock. Peter, the fisherman, now was to be Peter, the shepherd — the pastor of the Lord's flock.

As shepherd—pastor, Peter was to know each sheep by name, to guide them in right paths, to lead them to verdant pastures, to refresh their souls, to protect them from harm, to search out and return safely any who might stray, and to bring them to dwell in the house of the Lord.

As the first pastor of the flock of Jesus, Peter devoted the remainder of his life in faithful and loving care of the sheep of Jesus. As the flock grew and multiplied, other pastors called by Jesus joined to carry out the commission to feed His lambs and tend His sheep. In the end, like his Lord, Peter — the good shepherd — laid down his life for the flock of Jesus.

Through each age and in all parts of the world, shepherd—pastors continue to this day to tend and feed the flock of Jesus. There is, however, a serious problem which, like the cloud in Luke 12:54, is rising on the horizon. The cloud observed in this country extends, as well, over Europe and other parts of the world. It does not portend merely a rainy day. Rather, it threatens all of the sheep of Jesus and already seriously harms many flocks of Jesus across the United States.

The hope for the future is that today's shepherds in the United States, especially the principal shepherd— bishops, unlike the listeners to Jesus' words, will "know how to interpret the present time" and will take the necessary action to dissipate the threat of the cloud.

The National Conference of Catholic Bishops, through the Committee on Priestly Life and Ministry, took a major step in the process of seeking "to interpret the present time" when it commissioned the Center for Applied Research in the Apostolate to conduct *The Study of the Impact of Fewer Priests on the Pastoral Ministry.*

The results of the study, announced in June 2000, provide a clear image of the size and shape of the dark cloud which threatens in a few years to radically influence the number, structure and nature of parishes across the country.

Presently there are 19,181 parishes in the United States.[117] Of that number, one-fourth do not have a resident full-time pastor (2,386 parishes are priestless, another 2,334 are served by a part-time pastor, and 437 parishes are entrusted to someone other than a priest.)[118] What might the picture look like ten years from now as the total number of active priests continues to decrease through retirements, deaths and departures? How much greater will be the total number and percent of parishes that are priestless or, at best, share a pastor with one or more other parishes? In the next ten years how many parishes will be closed or consolidated because of the scarcity of shepherd—pastors? These questions await answers.

Among the pastoral strategies identified on page 197, only one, the establishment or increased support of a diocesan vocation office, has the potential to alleviate to any degree the growing shortage of priests. Many dioceses for years have had vocation offices which have not appreciably increased the pool of active priests. Yet it is essential that vocation efforts in each diocese continue and be enhanced.

The remaining pastoral strategies reported in the study are not designed to increase priestly vocations. Rather, they are designed to accommodate to an anticipated continuing decline in the number of priests.

Notably missing from the list of pastoral strategies is the one which comes first to the lips of the faithful when the subject of the shortage of priests is discussed. For at least four decades survey after survey has asked Catholics their view about married priests. Invariably, a large majority of respondents (71 percent in a recent survey[119]) support permitting married men to be ordained as priests. Because the evidence of support for married priests among the faithful has already been so well documented, the CARA study chose not to include the subject of married priests in its focal group discussions or telephone interviews.

Following a review of the CARA study at the June 15-17, 2000 Spring Meeting of the National Conference of Catholic Bishops, the members of the conference were requested to submit by August 1, 2000, to the Bishops' Committee on Priestly Life and Ministry proposed action items in response to the findings of the study. At this writing, information as to the nature and number of proposed action items submitted by the individual bishops is not available. It would be surprising, however, if any proposals included action items related to the married priesthood since the CARA study avoided the topic.

It would be regrettable if the NCCB drew solely upon the CARA study as a basis to "interpret the present time" phenomenon of a steadily diminishing number of priests. In addition to the survey data already mentioned, the NCCB has the powerful precedent of its own previous action on a matter directly related to the subject of married priests. As discussed in Chapter 3, the NCCB in 1979 petitioned the Holy See and on July 22, 1980 received permission from Pope John Paul II to ordain to the Catholic priesthood married former Episcopalian ministers. The permission, or pastoral provision, given at that time continues in effect to this day. A list of priests ordained under the pastoral provision appears on pages 98-100.

Following the leadership of the NCCB, the Canadian Conference of Bishops in 1986 and the Bishops' Conference of England and Wales in 1995 obtained from the Holy See pastoral provisions for their respective jurisdictions.

In addition to the pastoral provision, the NCCB has the example of some of its members who have obtained individual rescripts and have ordained as Catholic priests married former sacred ministers from the Methodist, Lutheran and Presbyterian traditions.

In each case to date in which a married former sacred minister of another Christian communion has been ordained as a Catholic priest, ordination has been conferred in recognition of the individual petitioner's spiritual journey into full communion with the Catholic church.

When one considers the subject of a married priesthood in the context of "the present time," the parameters of the discussion are very different. The question is not framed in the context of an action taken on behalf of a particular individual. Rather, the context is whether the ordination of married Catholic men should be permitted in the interest of the great pastoral needs of the Catholic faithful, particularly those who now do not have, or in the near future will not have, a resident pastor or reasonable access to mass and the sacraments. Presently the flocks of Jesus in thousands of parishes are without the leadership, counsel and Eucharistic ministry of a priest. In future years it will become increasingly difficult, without a significant increase in the number of priests, for the Church in the United States to carry out the mission given by Jesus to Peter: "Feed my lambs." "Tend my sheep." "Feed my sheep."

Where will the vocations come from?

As in the past, there always will be men who, having received the gift of a special charism, hear and respond to the call of Jesus to become celibate priests. But in what number? Will the pattern of several decades reverse and will the number of celibate priests ordained be sufficient to meet the pastoral needs of the steadily increasing flock of Jesus? In the period 1950-2000, the Catholic population grew at an annual rate of about two percent a year.[120] Meanwhile, the number of priests has not kept pace with this growth.

While not discounting the possibility of dramatic intervention by the Holy Spirit to greatly increase the number of future vocations to the celibate priesthood, a prudent "interpretation of the present time" should include thoughtful planning for a viable alternative. The option of having a priesthood consisting of both celibate and married priests, as in the Eastern Catholic Churches, offers such an alternative. Nor would such an alternative necessitate a change in the general law of canon 1042, 1°.

On this subject the *Ad Hoc* Committee Report to the CLSA of June 1, 1996 states:

> The issues addressed in this report apply to the present situations described above; they would also apply to any other situation in which the competent ecclesiastical authorities were to determine to permit the ordination of married men to the priesthood. Such a determination need not be for the entire Latin Church; in parallel with the provisions of the Eastern code (CCEO c. 758, §3), particular legislation could be authorized by the Apostolic See for individual episcopal conferences.[121]

Among the married male portion of nearly 64 million Catholics in the United States, how many men at some time in their lives have felt a call to the priesthood but did not respond because they had not received the charism of celibacy and felt called to the vocation of marriage and family life?

How many others after marriage and the fathering of children felt that they were called to the additional vocation of the priesthood?

While it might be easy to consider such questions as vain speculation, the questions should not be dismissed lightly. It is a matter of faith that the Holy Spirit breathes where and when he wills. Is it impossible that a call to the priesthood might come at any time, including after marriage? The history of the early Church, the unbroken tradition of the Eastern Catholic Churches, and, in recent years, the call to priesthood after marriage received by each of the priests ordained under the pastoral provision not only give ample witness to the compatibility of the vocations of priesthood and marriage but also show that the Holy Spirit is not bound by human laws as to the timing and order of the call to each person's vocation, or vocations.

The expansion of the married priesthood in the United States beyond the examples already discussed would require careful planning and preparation to initiate. The NCCB, however, has extensive experience in implementation and direction of both the highly successful permanent diaconate program and in the pastoral provision program. Much that has been learned through these two programs is transferable with appropriate adaptation to a broader acceptance of married priests.

The permanent diaconate program already has operational models is areas such as: formation outside of seminaries, the development of curriculum models and criteria to assess length of training and readiness to assume ministerial responsibilities, as well as experience with the training and role of wives.

Whatever the challenges to be overcome, the benefit of having a potentially great increase in the overall number of shepherd—pastors would greatly enhance the ability of the Church in future years to be faithful to the commission of Jesus to feed and tend the lambs and sheep of his flock in the United States.

At least three models exist whereby the possibility of ordination to the priesthood might become accessible to married Catholic men.

1. New Pastoral Provision

The National Conference of Catholic Bishops might petition the Holy See to grant a new pastoral provision in favor of the grave ministerial needs of the Catholic faithful resulting from the scarcity of celibate priests in the United States. Under the present pastoral provision, in response to the request of a sponsoring bishop, the Holy See may grant a dispensation from the simple impediment of canon 1042, 1° "a man who has a wife" to a married former Episcopal sacred minister who is a candidate for the Catholic priesthood. Once a rescript for ordination has been received, the sponsoring bishop may proceed to the ordination of the candidate when all other conditions established by the bishop have been satisfied.

The new pastoral provision would operate in a manner similar to the present pastoral provision, except that the candidate seeking ordination to the priesthood would be a married Catholic man, rather than a married former

Episcopal sacred minister. The rules presently in place might apply, where appropriate. For example, the candidate would need a sponsoring bishop who would express his intent to ordain the candidate to the priesthood following receipt of a rescript for ordination from the Holy See. In addition, under the new pastoral provision, the permission of the candidate's wife would be required and an appropriate course of study and formation for the priesthood would be established by the bishop depending upon the background of each candidate. Possibly, the period of study and formation might be integrated in some manner with the well-established system already developed for the permanent diaconate.

However, since the new pastoral provision would be sought in the interest of the ministerial needs of the Catholic faithful, not in response to the spiritual journey of an individual candidate, and, since there would be no danger of schism or heresy on the part of the married Catholic candidate, there would be no need for the new pastoral provision to include any restriction upon the nature of the assignment which might be undertaken after ordination. The bishop would have unrestricted authority to assign a priest ordained under the new pastoral provision to any assignment which normally might be given to other priests in the diocese, including an assignment to the "*cura animarum*" as pastor.

2. Code of Canons of the Eastern Churches (CCEO) Model

The National Conference of Catholic Bishops might request from the Holy See permission for the Latin Church in the United States to follow the options concerning celibacy or marriage provided for Eastern Catholic Churches in the CCEO canon 373:

> Clerical celibacy chosen for the sake of the kingdom of heaven and suited to the priesthood is to be greatly esteemed everywhere, as supported by the tradition of the whole Church; likewise, the hallowed practice of married clerics in the primitive Church and in the tradition of the Eastern Churches throughout the ages is to be held in honor.

Any married priest ordained under such a provision would be bound to the further requirement of the CCEO canon 375:

> In leading family life and in educating children married clergy are to show an outstanding example to other Christian faithful.

The advantage of a general permission of the nature contained in CCEO canon 373 would be that each bishop would have the authority to ordain suitable candidates, celibate or married, in his own diocese without the necessity of referral to the Holy See for permission in individual cases. Choice of this option, however, would bring forward the necessity for the hierarchy to address and rethink its prior position reflected in the decrees of the Holy See, *Cum data fuerit* and *Qua sollerti*, which opposed the presence of married priests of the Eastern Catholic Churches in the United States.

3. Support for the Actions of Individual Members of NCCB

The National Conference of Catholic Bishops might choose to refrain from any action of the entire body to request a general permission from the Holy See. Rather, the NCCB might resolve to provide fraternal support to brother bishop members who individually might seek from the Holy See dispensations from the simple impediment of canon 1042, 1° to permit the ordination of married Catholic men for their dioceses. This model parallels closely the actions of individual bishops who have petitioned the Holy See and received rescripts to permit the ordination of sacred ministers of Christian communions which are not embraced by the current pastoral provision, for example, married former ministers of the Methodist, Lutheran and Presbyterian churches.

Support, in this instance, might include the use of both personal and material resources available to the NCCB: to develop common guidelines for requesting dispensations on behalf of married Catholic men, to make available the expertise of staff in individual dioceses as needed by bishops who choose to seek permission from the Holy See, to assist in the development of curricula, and to prepare appropriate information and educational materials for the media and for the faithful.

Further Considerations

The three alternatives discussed above are not offered as the only ways in which married Catholic men might be introduced into the Catholic priesthood in the United States. Nor are the discussions as presented viewed as complete. At best, they offer initial ideas which would require additional serious study and development should any one or more of the models be elected.

One final consideration on the subject has to do with the potential number of candidates who might seek ordination to the priesthood if the NCCB sought and received from the Holy See permission to ordain to the priesthood married male Catholics in favor of the expanding pastoral needs of the rapidly increasing number of Catholics in the United States.

In May 1979[122] the National Conference of Catholic Bishops passed a resolution to seek permission from the Holy See to ordain married former Episcopal clergy who sought full communion with the Catholic Church and desired to continue their sacred ministry as Catholic priests. The NCCB took this historic action in response to the personal requests of a small band of fewer than 50 clergy[123] from another Christian communion.

The Holy See generously approved the request of the NCCB on July 22, 1980. Two years later on June 29, 1982, the first married former Episcopal clergyman, Father James Parker, was ordained a Catholic priest by then Bishop Bernard Law, the Ecclesiastic Delegate for the Pastoral Provision. The total number of priests ordained under the pastoral provision in the United States as of April 2000 was 73, including 61 married men and 12 men who were celibates. An additional few married former clergy of other Christian communions also have been ordained as Catholic priests.

Among the millions of male Catholics who are married or plan to marry are there not those who, like Peter and present-day married, former clergy of the Episcopal, Presbyterian, Methodist, and Lutheran communions, have heard the gentle call of Jesus: "Come follow me"? How many of their number might respond generously to meet the increasing shortage of priests, if given the opportunity?

As the National Conference of Catholic Bishops considers the implications arising from *The Study of the Impact of Fewer Priests on the Pastoral Ministry*, Catholics of the United States, who overwhelmingly support the ordination of married men, may hope and pray that a further study by the NCCB, or other interested researchers, will be undertaken to determine:

The Interest of Male Catholics Who Are Married or Plan to Marry in Ordination to the Priesthood and the Canonical and Practical Steps Necessary to Reestablish the Apostolic Tradition of Both Celibate and Married Priests as the General Norm of the Church.

EPILOGUE

The Siblings
A Parable About Priesthood Today

Betty and Roger

Betty was a beautiful young girl, a good student and everyone's friend. Roger knew more about cars than calculus. He barely got by in class but shone as an all-State running back. Betty and Roger had gone steady since junior year. In the fall of senior year Roger proposed and they decided to marry right after graduation. "No way," stormed Betty's dad, "you're going to college! He's a bum and will ruin your life."

Graduation day was special—an end and a beginning for Betty and Roger. After her parents were asleep, Betty slipped out the side door. Roger waited in the car. They drove across the state line and the next day found a justice to marry them.

Roger readily found a job at the track repairing and testing race cars. Betty waited on tables to help with the rent on their small apartment and to put a little aside for her "community college fund." Life was good.

The months passed. Then one Tuesday Betty received the news at work. There had been a crash at the track. The car burst into flames. Nothing could be done.

After the funeral Betty went back to work. She could not go home pregnant with Roger's baby. As the months went by, she worked longer hours to dull the pain of loneliness and just to get by financially. Then one night the pain became unbearable. It wasn't her time yet.

The ambulance arrived quickly and at the hospital the medics rolled her directly to the operating room. First one little boy the size of the doctor's hand claimed his place in the world. Then the little girl, followed by two more boys. Nurses rushed the infants to neonatal intensive care while the doctors worked to stop Betty's hemorrhage. Nothing could be done. She passed quietly to rejoin Roger.

The nurses named the infants: Baby Boy 1 : Leo, Baby Girl : Rebecca, Baby Boy 2 : Martin, Baby Boy 3 : Joseph. Four months passed before the doctor released the infants to social service. With no next of kin, they were put up for adoption. Social service tried to keep them together, but in the small, economically depressed town no adoptive family came forward.

A national agency with a list of couples waiting to adopt offered to assist. The agency rationalized that it would be best to make four families happy, rather than try to find one family to take all of the infants. Thus began the stories of Leo Tawil, Rebecca Paquet, Martin Sexton and Joseph Lally.

Leo's Story

Doctor and Mrs. Charles Tawil were a loving couple who had been blessed in many ways but had been childless until God sent them Leo. The deep faith of the Tawils as Melkite Catholics offered Leo a steady beacon in his youth and early manhood. His father was a model of the man Leo hoped to become: a man of deep faith in and love of God, of total commitment to his family and church, of unstinting generosity to those most in need of his service.

Leo took the first step on his journey to follow his father's path when he entered Harvard and began a pre-medicine curriculum. He pursued his courses diligently and with academic success. Along the way, he met Nancy, a fellow student, whom he soon realized was to be much more in his life. As they shared the secrets of their hearts, Leo revealed that he felt torn between his attraction to the medical profession and a deeper call which he felt to the priesthood.

Nancy, an Italian Catholic, was dismayed by Leo's revelation, until Leo clarified that the Melkite church accepted married men as candidates for the priesthood. In time Leo resolved his professional conflict and with the support of Nancy applied to be received as a candidate for the priesthood.

While Nancy continued her medical education, Leo began the seminary training in philosophy and theology required to become a priest. Some months before his ordination to the diaconate, Leo and Nancy married. The following year, as the bishop placed his hands upon Leo's head and ordained him to the priesthood in the Melkite Catholic Church, Nancy sat in the front row of the church, Leo Jr. nestled in her arms.

Rebecca's Story

Rebecca was the smallest of the siblings at birth but quickly gained strength in the hospital nursery. By the time George and Lucy Paquet took her home as their daughter, she was a bright, beautiful and very determined little girl. The Paquets had been inactive Catholics for much of their lives. The coming of Rebecca changed that.

The little infant who charmed them at first sight rekindled in their hearts a flame of love and gratitude toward God which glowed over the years. They praised the miracle of God's grace as Rebecca developed into a caring young person and a soul constantly in search of God's purpose in her own life. She moved with grace, always extending herself to embrace the promise of the next moment.

George and Lucy were the proudest of parents as Rebecca captained her high school soccer team to a league championship and as she crossed the stage to deliver the valedictory address at graduation. When George died during Rebecca's junior year at college, Rebecca left school to be with her mother. For two years mother and daughter lived and prayed together until Lucy insisted that Rebecca resume her studies and pursue the journey of her own life.

Drawn by prayer and reading, and assisted in her discernment by a wise spiritual guide, Rebecca chose a course of studies consistent with a still distant call which gradually became clearer each year. At 23 years of age she earned a master's degree in religious education. At 26 she completed her dissertation and received a doctorate in theology from the Catholic University of America. Over the next five years she published three well-respected theological volumes, held office in the Catholic Theological Society of America, served as president of her parish council, and twice each week volunteered to care for hospice patients.

With each passing year the call grew clearer and more urgent until she no longer could ignore or deny it. "Rebecca, follow me. Feed my lambs. Tend my sheep." Now certain as to the voice and the meaning of the call, Rebecca extended herself once more to embrace the promise of the next moment.

"Father Ed," she explained to her spiritual guide, "God is calling me to become a priest. How shall I proceed?"

"Rebecca," the wise old spiritual guide advised, "at the present time the institutional Church does not acknowledge that God may call women to the priesthood. Pray that God may inspire the Church to recognize the vocation that He has given to you."

Martin's Story

Martin had the even-tempered disposition of a third child. The Reverend Robert Sexton and his wife Eunice were middle-aged when they adopted the chubby-faced infant who slept peacefully through the whole process as he was handed about from one person to another. Martin let it be known from the beginning that he would not be ruffled by the small brush fires of life.

It was not that Martin was dull, let alone dense. Rather, he had a surplus to deal with the vagaries of life. In preschool, if a playmate appropriated his favorite toy, Martin simply turned to another toy. Later, throughout his school years, Martin's calm manner often cast him as the mediator of conflicts among his friends, as the one who brought common sense to an inflamed situation.

When the appropriate time came, he announced without fanfare his decision to enter the Methodist ministry. He pursued an undergraduate philosophy degree at Boston University with respectable, if not outstanding, success. He had no difficulty in being accepted into the School of Theology where his well-balanced personality and solid spiritual values served him well. He completed his Bachelor of Divinity *cum laude*, received ordination, and accepted appointment as associate pastor at a suburban parish. He enjoyed parish ministry and chose a major in Christian ethics when he continued his studies for an STM, Master of Theology, degree.

Marriage to Margaret and the start of a family completed the circle of his life — or so he thought. As pastor of a modest sized parish in Boston, Martin became active in ecumenical activities, involving pulpit exchanges with other pastors, including the Catholic priest as St. Martha's. In time, Martin felt strongly drawn toward Catholicism and began conversations with the pastor at St. Martha's. The pastor encouraged Martin's interest and put him in touch with the director of priestly formation for the archdiocese to learn more about the possibility of ordination as a married Catholic priest.

Two years later, Martin prostrated himself at the feet of the Archbishop of Boston and rose at ceremony's end as an ordained Catholic priest of the Archdiocese, the husband of Margaret, and father of baby Jennifer.

Joseph's Story

Our Lady of Good Counsel held many memories for Joseph Lally. His adoptive parents brought him there directly from the hospital and dedicated his life to the Blessed Mother. He had received Baptism, First Communion, and Confirmation there. Daily he had been an altar boy for the 8:00 a.m. mass in the ornate church before rushing to his classes at the adjacent parochial school. Father McCabe, the pastor, was loved by all, but by none more than the parish altar boys who were his special favorites.

Later for Joseph there had been Catholic High School and College, Georgetown Law, marriage to Ann at Good Counsel and, in time, the four children, each a unique gift of God. Joseph treasured his faith which gave meaning to everything in his life and which deepened over the years as he and Ann grew ever closer in their oneness with one another and with Jesus.

He devoted much of his practice to *pro bono* cases, served as Eucharistic minister, and was moderator of the adult scripture program. Yet there was more. The call which had beckoned him during college revived and would not be denied. As a college junior he had found himself deeply in love with the woman whom God had given to be his soul-mate and he also had felt strongly drawn to the priesthood.

Pray as he might, he was unable to reconcile the irreconcilable. His confessor told him that the Church did not permit married priests. He admonished him that only those brave enough to give up the pleasures of family life for a life of celibate sacrifice were worthy to become priests. Joseph could not imagine a life of perpetual celibacy. Growing up he had daily witness of the beautiful bond of love between his adoptive parents, the constant showering of their love on him, and their constant sacrifices on his behalf. Reluctantly, he repressed any thought of becoming a priest, until, after all the years, the call broke through the layers of repression to summon him once again.

He discussed his feelings with Ann who understood and supported him. They left the children with Ann's mother for a week and went on retreat. Joseph had heard about some married former Episcopalian ministers who had been ordained as Catholic priests, but he could not find any solid information on the subject. The director of the retreat house proved helpful. A priest friend of his was a married convert from the Episcopal church and he arranged for Joseph to meet him.

The married former Episcopalian told Joseph of all the difficulties he had encountered to be ordained under the pastoral provision but assured Joseph that it was worth all of the bureaucratic hassle. Unfortunately, he said, Joseph was ineligible for ordination under the pastoral provision because he already was Catholic. Joseph could not believe that his

Catholic faith could be the obstacle which prevented him from ordination.

He was discouraged, but understood more clearly that the requirement of celibacy was not of divine origin. It was simply a matter of canon law. As a lawyer, Joseph knew that the laws of man allowed for changes, or for exceptions — as the pastoral provision proved. He determined to take his case to his former pastor, now Bishop McCabe.

Bishop McCabe welcomed Joseph with a warm embrace. "I'm always pleased to see one of my boys. How are Ann and the children? What brings you here?"

Joseph spoke openly of his personal spiritual journey, ending with the question: "Bishop McCabe, is there any hope? Is there any way in which I can become a priest?"

"Joseph, I'm surprised," Bishop McCabe answered. "As one of my boys, a special one, I might add, I expect you to remember that hope is one of the three theological virtues. There is always hope. In my view, you would make a very fine candidate for ordination to the priesthood. That is, if we can get around the small matter of canon 1042, 1°."

"What is that?" Joseph asked.

"A church rule," Bishop McCabe explained, "one that prohibits a married man from being ordained without a special dispensation from the Holy See. It doesn't apply to the Eastern churches, of course. They always have permitted married priests. The rule only applies to the Latin church. To date, the Holy See has given dispensations to former Protestant ministers from a number of denominations. I have two married priests in the diocese, one a former Episcopalian and the other a former Lutheran. I would welcome others. I have even a few priests from abroad. Still, it is not enough. Right now I have seven parishes without a priest. And last year I had to close two parishes because of the priest shortage.

The difficulty in your case, Joseph, is that the Holy See has yet to grant a dispensation from the marriage impediment to a married Catholic lay man. Actually, I don't know if any bishop has even asked for one.

That will be the plan, Joseph. You will have to work with a canon lawyer that I will assign to build up the strongest case possible to present to the Holy See. You will have to cooperate fully. You must realize that it may take time, and require additional studies and other things on your part. And Ann will have to support your request. She does, doesn't she?"

"Wholeheartedly, Bishop."

"Good, that is very important. Joseph, I am very pleased that you came to see me. The diocese is facing a severe crisis due to the lack of priests. You ask if there is

239

hope. There is always hope, if we do our part. I will personally deliver my request for a rescript for your ordination to the Holy Father. We must have hope, and we must pray. We must pray and trust in the Good Shepherd."

DOCUMENTS LIST

ENDNOTES

1.   Meir Bar-Ilan, http://faculty.biu.acil/barilm/

2.   Catholic Encyclopedia, St. Peter, Prince of the Apostles.

3.   Catholic Encyclopedia, St. Peter, Prince of the Apostles.

4.   Catholic Encyclopedia, Celibacy of the clergy.

5.   Catholic Encyclopedia, St. Philip.

6.   Pope Paul VI, *Sacerdotalis caelibatus,* June 24, 1967, par. 5, 17.

7.   Diez, G. Martinez & F. Rodriguez, *La coleccion canonica hispana,* Madrid, 1984, IV, p. 253.

8.   Percoval, Henry R. ed. *The Seven Ecumenical Councils of the Undivided Church,* repr. Edinburgh: T&T Clark; Grand Rapids, MI: Wm. B. Eerdmans, 1988.

9.   Catholic Encyclopedia, Celibacy of the clergy.

10. *Epist. Ad Rusticum Narbonensem episcopum. Inquis. III Resp. PL 54, 1204a.*

11. The Canons of the Council of Trullo, http://www.ccel.org/fathers/NPNF2-1416 trullo/canon3.

12. Catholic Encyclopedia, Pope St. Hormisas.

13. Catholic Encyclopedia, Pope Ardian II.

14. Catholic Encyclopedia, Pope St. Gregory VII.

15. *Medieval Sourcebook: Ninth Ecumenical Council: Lateran I, 1123, The Canons of the First Lateran Council*

16. *Medieval Sourcebook: Tenth Ecumenical Council: Lateran II, 1139, The Canons of the Second Lateran Council.*

17. *Council of Trent, Twenty-Third Session, http://history.hanover.edu/early/trent/ct 24 matt.htm.*

18. *Council of Trent, Twenty-Fourth Session, http://history.hanover.edu/early/trent/ct 24 matt.htm.*

19. *Decree on the Catholic Churches of the Eastern Rite (Orientalium Ecclesiarum),* Pope Paul VI, November 21, 1964.

20. *Decree on the Ministry and Life of Priests (Presbyterorum Ordinis).* Pope Paul VI, December 7, 1965.

21. Fichter, Joseph, *The Pastoral Provisions : Married Catholic Priests,* Sheed & Ward, Kansas City, Mo., 1989.

22. Hill, Richard A., *Ordination of Married Protestant Ministers* in Proceedings of the Fifty-First Annual Convention of the Canon Law Society of America, Seattle, Wa., Oct. 9-12, 1989, p.95.

23. Donovan, Mary S., *Women as Priests,* UALR History Seminar, November 7, 1989. Revised July 20, 1992.

24. *Canons of the Episcopal Church, Title III — Ministry, CANON 4: Of Postulants for Holy Orders.*

25. Fichter, p. 29.

26. Fichter, p. 31.

27. Fichter, p. 74.

28. Pope Leo XIII, *Apostolicae Curae.*

29. Fichter, p.1, p.3.

30. *Origins,* Vol. 10: No. 43, p.674.

31. *Origins,* Vol. 11, No. 33, p. 517.

32. Dally, Mary Vincent, *Married To A Catholic Priest — A Journey of Faith.* Loyola Press, Chicago, 1988.

33. Stetson, William, Secretary to Cardinal Law for the Pastoral Provision, Letter to author of April 7, 2000.

34. Stetson, letter.

35. Hill, p. 100.

36. Stetson, letter.

37. Our Lady of the Atonement
     http://www. atonementonline.com

38. Phillips, Christopher, G., Letter to author of February 28, 2000.

39. Our Lady of Walsingham
     http://web.net/-nccsa186/walsingham.htm.

40. Fichter, p. 49.

41. St. Mary the Virgin
    http://rampages.omra.net/-eleison/

42. Congregation of St. Athanasius
    http://www.locutor.net.

43. www.pastoralprovision.org.

44. Stetson. letter.

45. Hill, p. 99.

46. Fichter, Gallup, others.

47. Ratzinger, Joseph, letter of December 15, 1986.

48. Pope Paul VI, *Sacerdotalis caelibatus, n. 42, 1967.*

49. Ratzinger, letter of April 13, 1992.

50. Complete text of the Process is given at page 113 ff.

51. Hill, p. 100.

52. Complete text of the Guidelines is given at p. 119 ff.

53. Anglican Church of England, General Synod, July 2000.

54. Catholic Bishops' Conference of England and Wales, Letter to author of January 19, 2000.

55. htpp://rampages.net/-eleison/leonard.htm.

56. Fichter, p. 68.

57. Giles, John H. Jr.,My Journey to Married Catholic Priesthood, January, 1998

58. http://www.seattletimes.com/extra/browse/html/altca th-122296.html.

59. http://www.seattletimes.com/extra/browse/html/altca th-122296.html.

60. http://www.austindiocese.org/spirit-heimsoth.htm.

61. http://www.pioneer.com/sevendays/3/news/docs/034 866.htm

62. Telephone interview with author, August 2001

63. http://www.SMMP.com/Bulletin Archives/B-000820.htm

64. newera@in.co.za.

65. http://churchnet.ucsm.ac.uk/news/file2/news397.htm

66. *Decree on the Catholic Churches of the Eastern Rite (Orientalium Ecclesiarum)*, promulgated by Pope Paul VI on November 21, 1964.

67. Roberson, Ronald, *The Eastern Catholic Churches, A Brief Survey, 6th edition, Edizioni Orientalia Christians, Pontificio Instituto Orientale, Roma, Italy*, pp. 143-188.

68. CCEO, p. xv.

69. CCEO, p. 737.

70. *Cum Data Fuerit*, March 1, 1929 (AAS 1929, 152 ss.)

71. *Qua Sollerti*, December 23, 1929, (AAS 1930, 99-105).

72. *The Norms of Particular Law of the Byzantine Metropolitan Church Sui Juris of Pittsburgh, U.S.A.*, October 1, 1999.

73. Stasiuk, Peter, Melbourne, Australia, Press Release http://byzcath.org/news/98-Australia.htm.

74. AAS 59 (1967), pp. 697-704.

75. AAS 64 (1972), pp. 534-540.

76. *Supplementary Document "D", The Study of the Impact of Fewer Priests on the Pastoral Ministry*, National Conference of Catholic Bishops, Spring General Meeting, June 15-17, 2000 Milwaukee, WI.

77. *Document "D"*, Introduction, p. ii.

78. *Document "D"*, p. 17.

79. *Document "D"*, p. 19.

80. *Document "D"*, p. iv.

81. *Document "D"*, p. 22.

82. *Document "D"*, p. 29.

83. *Document "D"*, p. 27.

84. *Document "D"*, p. 30.

85. *Document "D"*, p. 18.

86. *Document "D"*, p. 29.

87.   *Document "D"*, p. 20.

88.   *Document "D"*, p. 32.

89.   *Document "D"*, pp. vi, 37.

90.   *Document "D"*, p. 15.

91.   *Document "D"*, p. 14.

92.   *Document "D"*, p. 37.

93.   *National Catholic Reporter,* June 30, 2000, p.5.

94.   *Document "D"*, p. 29.

95.   *Document "D"*, p. 30.

96.   *Document "D"*, p. 29.

97.   Young, Lawrence, A., Assessing and Updating the Schoenherr-Young Projections of Clergy Decline in the United States Roman Catholic Church, *Sociology of Religion,* 1998, 59:17-23.

98.   The Permanent Diaconate Today, CARA Special Report, June 2000, p. 1.

99. The Permanent Diaconate Today, CARA Special Report, June 2000, p. 2.

100. *Document "D"*, p. 34 ff.

101. American Catholics Survey, Table 13, *National Catholic Reporter,* October 29, 1999.

102. Resoution 4: CLSA *Proceedings* 32 (1970) 106-107.

103. "Priestly Ministry and Celibacy in the United States," *The Jurist 32* (1972), 273-289.

104. Resolution 8: CLSA *Proceedings* 49 (1987) 371-372.

105. Hill, Richard A, "The Pastoral Provision: Ordination of Married Protestant Ministers," CLSA *Proceedings* 51 (1989) 95-100.

106. Ward, Daniel, "Presidential Report," CLSA *Proceedings* 54 (1992) 208.

107. Coriden, James A. & James H. Provost, *Canonical Implications Related to the Ordination of Married Men to the Priesthood in the United States, Ad Hoc Committee Report* to CLSA, June 1, 1996, Introduction.

108. *Ad Hoc Committee Report,* Introduction.

109. *Ad Hoc Committee Report*, Entrance into Sacred Ministry, 1. Discernment of Vocation.

110. *Ad Hoc Committee Report*, Entrance into Sacred Ministry, 1. Discernment of Vocation.

111. *Ad Hoc Committee Report*, Entrance into Sacred Ministry, 2. Formation for Ministry.

112. *Ad Hoc Committee Report*,. Entrance into Sacred Ministry, 3. Irregularities and Impediments.

113. *Ad Hoc Committee Report*, Entrance into Sacred Ministry, 3. Irregularities and Impediments.

114. *Ad Hoc Committee Report*, Obligations and Rights of Clergy, 2, Continence and Celibacy.

115. *Ad Hoc Committee Report*, Obligations and Rights of Clergy, 4. Financial Support.

116. *Ad Hoc Committee Report*, Obligations and Rights of Clergy, 5. Benefits.

117. *Document "D"*, p. 4.

118. *Document "D"*, p. 37.

119. *National Catholic Reporter*, June 30, 2000, p. 5.

120. *Document "D"*, p. 4.

121. *Ad Hoc Committee Report*, Introduction.

122. Fichter, p. 31.

123. In the fall of 1981, Bishop Law convened a three-day orientation and training meeting in Dallas which was attended by 26 petitioners (p.77)